From The Projects to *Profiles*

A Memoir

Mickey Burns

NEW HAVEN PUBLISHING

From the Projects to *Profiles*

First Edition
Published 2019
NEW HAVEN PUBLISHING LTD
www.newhavenpublishingltd.com
newhavenpublishing@gmail.com

Cover design ©Pete Cunliffe
pcunliffe@blueyonder.co.uk

newhaven
publishing

ISBN: 978-1-912587-26.1

**To all the children of the
South Beach Projects,
past, present and future;
dream big and work hard to make
those dreams come true**

To Michael & Todd,
Hope you enjoy my
Memoir... In gratitude,
Mickey

P.S. Please take Michael on
more trips!!!

Table of Contents

Introduction

I love being a television host - what could be better than sitting down with celebrities to discuss their lives and careers? I've been doing exactly that for over two decades, and I have yet to love it any less now than I did the day I started. Every new interview brings new challenges and excitement.

In 2009, I had television creator Chuck Barris as a guest on *Profiles*. He told me then, 'Mickey, you have a book in you.' Since then, it has been a goal of mine to get to writing it; I finally have, and it (thankfully) hasn't been as painstaking as I originally thought it might be.

So I decided to write a memoir and start from the beginning, because to truly appreciate where we are today, we must first understand the roots from which we evolve.

I grew up in the South Beach Housing Projects, on Staten Island, in the 1950s and 1960s. I want to start out by explaining how those experiences gave me the mental toughness and drive that helped me succeed throughout my life. I'm convinced, had I not grown up in the projects, that my life would certainly have taken a different path. It taught me how to survive, and how to put in the work for anything and everything you set out to accomplish. I owe much to the South Beach Projects. I also want to write about my broadcasting career while sharing many of my most cherished memories of the celebrities that I've had the honor to have interviewed. My celebrity interview series *Profiles* has been on the air in the New York City Tri-State area for nearly twenty years now, as we inch closer to our 500th episode milestone. It's been quite a ride. A reporter recently asked me if I had a favorite episode. My answer was, 'I think there was something special and unique within each and every one of our nearly 500 episodes.' So, in this book, I hope to share many of the stories that have made my life, and my show, so rewarding.

As I reflect, I think back to our first interview, with musician Chuck Mangione, who was kind enough to explain to me the difference between a flugelhorn and a trumpet. I then flashed forward to our 100th episode with talk show host Dick Cavett, who reminded me that he and Johnny Carson were both from Nebraska, which, according to Mr. Cavett, was a prerequisite to being a successful talk show host. I clearly remember sitting in singer Teddy Pendergrass's living room in Philadelphia, waiting for him to join me for our interview. In a wheelchair, paralyzed from the neck down, he was wheeled in by an assistant across from me for the interview. I remember thinking, *What a tragedy, and what courage this man has to keep persevering the way he has.* I fondly remember my two interviews with comedian Joan Rivers, who repeatedly said during our time together, 'You're really a great interviewer', giving me enormous confidence beyond description. I'll never forget walking up Broadway with legendary master actor Eli Wallach after our *Profiles* interview; he was headed for a shoe repair shop. When I asked Mr. Wallach 'Why not just go out and buy a new pair?' he stopped me, mid-stride and said, 'I grew up in the Depression. Back then, we never bought new - we fixed old, and I've never been able to shake that.' Our 300th episode also comes to mind, with actress Susan Lucci, whose hair, on the day of our interview, was not cooperating due to the hot lights and an air conditioning malfunction, and she knew it. However, as the consummate professional that she is, she never said a word, and never complained. Instead, she showed us all the elegance of a polished pro. Most recently, ballerina Misty Copeland walked onto our set and approached every crew member with a big smile, shook everyone's hand and warmly introduced herself. In doing so, she reminded us what the true definition of class is.

Many years ago - I think it was in the late 1970s - a friend of mine presented me with a neatly wrapped birthday gift. As I was opening the gift I quickly realized that it was a book. I remember the cover to be bright yellow, and the title read: *Everything I Know About Coaching* by Mickey Burns. When I opened the book, I laughed when I realized all the pages were blank! My ultimate hope for those who read my current book, *From The Projects To Profiles*, is that they will find this to be a bit more interesting and compelling.

- Mickey Burns

From the Projects to *Profiles*

Foreword by Bonnie Humphrey, Ph.D. President Missouri Valley College

As President of Mickey Burn's alma mater, it is an honor to offer a foreword to this book by and about one of our most distinguished alumni and a cherished friend.

To speak plainly, sometimes you run across people in your life and even before you know them really well, you can just tell they are special. In my 15 of years as President of Missouri Valley College, I have met some very special people. Mickey Burns is at the top of that list. Asked to describe Mickey, I would use the words upbeat, professional, loyal and resolute to always give his best effort no matter the task.

In this tumultuous world, I have never seen Mickey Burns when he was not in a happy, upbeat mood. He loves life and always tries to live it to the fullest. Any time I have asked Mickey to help me with something regarding the college or our students, there was never any hesitation. His reply has always been - "Let's do it!"

I have also seen Mickey in several social situations and he never lets go of his professionalism, or his human compassion. One time in particular, I had another colleague with me on a business trip to Manhattan in mid-December. Mickey and several other Missouri Valley College alumni were having dinner with me in a crowded downtown Manhattan restaurant. The atmosphere was festive and we were all laughing and enjoying each other's company. Our colleague was "over-served" and things began to deteriorate. Mickey never missed a beat. He kept his professionalism in tact and helped me end the dinner with dignity and moved the gentleman along to keep from spoiling a lovely evening.

Loyalty to his friends and family is deeply ingrained in Mickey's heart. He has worn his class ring from Missouri Valley College every day since the day he received it many years ago. He has worn it so long that it is getting thin and the name of the college can barely be seen. I once asked him about it and he told me he has worn it proudly every day because the college helped shape his life. He is proud of it and very loyal to what it represents, even when there are countless newer, flashier and much more "status oriented" rings out there.

Mickey Burns is very professional and very resolute and always gives his best effort. He exhibited his best effort while coaching high school basketball, and he has continued to give his best effort every day during his television career. Preparation - preparation - preparation. Two things you can always count on: Mickey Burns will be totally professional and Mickey Burns will be very prepared.

Mickey's has been the life of an athlete, a coach, and a television visionary and pioneer. Everyone has a life story. This book tells Mickey's . . . and it's a great story! He is not only a successful professional, he is a good man.

Mickey Burns is a Missouri Valley Viking through and through. He and what he has done in his life is why colleges like ours exist. As President of his alma mater – and as his friend – it is an honor to pay tribute to him. Valley Will Roll!

Bonnie Humphrey, Ph.D.
President Missouri Valley College
Marshall, Missouri

October 1, 2019

Chapter 1
South Beach Living

My life changed in many ways when, in 1958, my family moved into a first-floor apartment in the South Beach Housing Projects, which was located a couple of miles from where the Verrazano Bridge now stands.

From the day we moved in, I immediately felt that this move would be a special, defining period in my life. Looking out my bedroom window, I could see, a stone's throw away, the elementary school that I would be attending. It was Public School 46; a massive building to my eleven-year-old eyes. However, what really stood out for me were the athletic fields that surrounded the school, both dirt fields and concrete playgrounds. My dad was a major league talent as a baseball player until World War II put an end to his making it to the big leagues. However, without a doubt, I had inherited his athletic genes. As far back as I can remember, my love of all sports ran deep, and much of my adolescence was spent playing the sport of the season. Baseball in the summer, football in the fall, and basketball in the winter.

Growing up in the South Beach Projects was a utopia for a kid like me. I would go to school across the dirt baseball field, then run home and change into my play clothes, which would normally consist of jeans, Joe Lapchick high top black sneakers, and a sweatshirt; then off to the playground I went! The best part of growing up in the South Beach Projects was that there were fifty to a hundred kids to play with, each and every day. We all seemed to have the same routine: school, change, then to the park to play till Mom called you home for dinner. She would do so by yelling out of our living room window, which faced the ball fields: 'Mickey, it's time for dinner! Come home!' Now, as I reminisce, it seems sort of amazing that we all actually trained ourselves to hear our own mother's voice calling us home from about a mile away.

Once in the playground, the kids would quickly choose up teams to compete in whatever the sport was for that season. If you didn't get to the playground fast enough, you waited on the field and called next, having to watch and then replace the losing team competing in the first game.

A couple of miles east of the projects lay the South Beach boardwalk, which I learned early on had a rich history. In the early 20th century, the neighborhood was full of summer bungalows, thanks to a beachfront lined with amusements, theaters, arcades, and rides. Families came from Manhattan, as well as the entire Tri-state region, to enjoy the festive resort community and, as it was known back then, The Franklin D. Roosevelt Boardwalk. South Beach was actually known as the 'Riviera of New York City' at the end of the century. My parents told me that the South Beach shore thrived through the 1920s, but the Great Depression, along with fires and water pollution, eventually got the best of the boardwalk and the community. The boardwalk area became rundown and neglected through the 1950s and 1960s, and this was the reality I grew up witnessing.

Nevertheless, as adolescents growing up in the South Beach Projects, my friends and I would take a mile or so walk down to the beach and enjoy the ocean during hot summer days. Mind you, there was never a shortage of posted signs to indicate that the water was well polluted. But what were a few hazard warnings to the youth! For young men, tenacious and invincible, that was as good a sign as any to jump right in and have a ball. Reflecting back, I can't ever remember becoming ill from any of our swims. In the late 90s, the South Beach waterfront began to flourish once again. The boardwalk was repaired and modernized, sports fields were created, and year-round fishing piers were constructed. However, on October 29th, 2012 South Beach was considered to be the epicenter of where Hurricane

Sandy came ashore and was hit extremely hard. People along the shore were lost, and the real estate damage was catastrophic. It's taken nearly a decade, but the area has since bounced back and may yet see its glory days once again.

I clearly remember that even the harshest of winters didn't deter us. After ice and snow events, the park supervisor, Fred Herman, would lend us his ice breaker. We would head down the outdoor basketball courts and start breaking up and clearing the ice and snow around the key near the basket, just enough to be able to conduct two-on-two games. Because we played through the winter, the tips of our fingers would have little splits. They were painful, but nothing a few band-aids couldn't cure. I'm not sure exactly why it was, but my friends and I *hated* to be indoors, and we only stayed in when the weather looked like it might kill us - and even then, we might've tried to push for a game or two anyway.

The opportunities for activities were unlimited, including nights between 6pm and 9pm, when the gym at Public School 46 became our night recreational center. It was open throughout the winter. Some nights offered free play, other nights they ran organized games. The one problem with the night center was that I always wanted to be there, instead of at home, doing homework and concentrating on my studies. It was a constant battle with Mom. However, reflecting back, she was absolutely right - my studies should have come first, not the night center. *Yes, Mom, you were right.*

Back in the late 1950s, the one thing everyone in the South Beach Projects had in common was that literally no one had any money. Most families had just enough to pay the rent and buy food, clothes, and other necessities. I don't ever remember anyone from the projects going on vacation. Where I came from, a vacation meant, 'I'm off from work for a few days.' The closest I ever got to Mexico and the Caribbean, in those days, was the world map on the wall in my bedroom. Going out to eat was a rarity. We did so only on special occasions, such as birthdays, anniversaries and graduations. Even then, it was nothing fancy, most likely a great hamburger at a middle of the road restaurant. In those days, every family seemed to be in the same boat. We were all short on material things and money; and yet, everyone appeared to be happy. As baby boomers of parents who experienced even tougher times during and after World War II, life was good, and to 'keep up with the Joneses' was not so evident in my neighborhood.

Most of our fathers had fought in World War II. My dad had served in the Army and spent a period of the time fighting in the Philippines. Instead of going off to college as I did, my father and millions of other young men and women went overseas and battled the two most powerful military machines ever assembled in the biggest war in the history of humankind. It was a war fought on six of the seven continents, and when it was over, 50 million had perished. We are the inheritors of everything they fought for, and that so many died for. My dad never made it to college, but he always hoped that I would. After the war, when they returned home in their late 20s or early 30s, they all were starting late with families and careers. In the early 50s, my dad got a city job as a bus driver. Back then, his salary was modest, but it was a steady job with health insurance and a pension down the road.

My dad was a drinker, a smoker, and a gambler. He was always the life of the party. However, his addictions made life difficult within the Burns household. Would we have enough food on the table? Would the rent be paid this month? These were the questions that myself, my brother Mark, and my mother Dorothy had to live with on a consistent basis.

My mother was an angel. She was totally devoted to her two sons and raised us with as much love and care as anyone could aspire to. She did the best she could in spite of my dad's addictions. Eventually, she took a job as an EKG technician to uplift the family's financial situation.

We became resourceful. The sneakers we wore, mostly Joe Lapchick high tops, would always wear out rather quickly because most of our games were played on concrete. The soles of the sneakers constantly wore down. The results were little holes, or at least they started out as little holes, on the soles. With each day and continued wear and tear, the holes got a little bigger. To extend the life of the sneakers we would cut out thick cardboard in the shape of the sneakers and insert them within. Think DIY, MacGyver-issued Scholl's inserts. This would get us another couple of weeks out of the sneakers before the hole got so big we may as well have been running on bare feet.

We recently had chef and television personality Andrew Zimmern as a guest on *Profiles*. His show *Bizarre Foods* has taken him to over 175 countries, where he showcases unique and interesting people and their stories, using food as the catalyst. Andrew was telling me a story about spending 10 days with the Bushmen in the Kalahari in Africa. As he was preparing dinner with the people in the village, they first worked together weaving rope from weeds and reeds they had gathered. Andrew was given and utilized some twine that he needed for the dish he was making. At one point, Andrew attempted to cut and throw away the excess twine in the garbage, to the dismay of the native people, who saw that as a character flaw. In their culture, they didn't throw anything away, but rather reused it again and again, until it became totally and utterly unusable. Andrew's story transformed me back to my childhood in the South Beach Projects and my Joe Lapchick high top sneakers. With the same wisdom, we, too, used those old sneakers every day, again and again, until they became totally and utterly unusable.

In retrospect, it really was a kid's heaven growing up in the South Beach Projects. Back then, there were no drugs, no computers, and no video games – just a bunch of kids having fun together while learning interpersonal skills each and every day.

Many of my contemporaries, with whom I grew up in the projects, today seem resistant to tell people about growing up there. I think for them it represents poverty, lack of education, and low income. None of which looks good on a resume when you're climbing the career ladder at a Wall Street firm. However, I felt just the opposite and wore my growing up in the projects as a badge of honor. I felt this way for a number of reasons. First off, to make it and survive as a kid growing up in the projects, you needed to learn a degree of toughness. You learned early on that nothing was going to come easy. Reflecting back, you had to fight for pretty much everything. There were no handouts, no silver spoons, no connections. If you wanted to achieve something, you learned early on that, if you wanted to get it done, you would have to do it for yourself, and you didn't look for help of any kind from anyone. It was almost akin to a 'you against the world' philosophy.

Remember John Travolta walking down the street in Brooklyn at the beginning of *Saturday Night Fever*? As kids from the South Beach Projects, we all walked that way - chip on the shoulder, swagger, and most importantly, with attitude.

No one gave us confidence, we learned it!

That toughness I learned growing up in the projects was an asset throughout my life. The most important thing it taught me was to never give up. In my world, giving up was never an option, regardless of the task. When I reflect back, I can't think of a single thing that I've ever given up on.

It just isn't in my South Beach Projects DNA.

I always felt that giving up on anything was like taking a step backward. Giving up also meant that the opportunity I was giving up on might never come my way again. Once I decided to take on a specific task, I was ALL-IN until its conclusion.

Chapter 2
Sports

By the time I was 13, I had evolved into one of the best athletes, not only in Public School 46, but, more importantly, in the South Beach Projects!

My athletic prowess had afforded me a great deal of respect amongst my peers. This respect not only kept me safe from the project's bullies, but made me a popular first choice when being picked for teams.

At my graduation ceremony in the spring of 1961 from PS 46, I was presented with a beautiful trophy for being voted the school's best athlete. For me, that honor was just as meaningful as if I had won the Heisman Trophy, which is the most prestigious award in college sports. That award also represented that if I continued to work hard - and I mean REALLY HARD - then maybe there would be more awards and trophies in my future.

From an early age, I saw sports as my way out of the projects, and quite possibly to a college education that I was sure would afford me unlimited possibilities. I would often ask my mother, 'Mom, how do you feel about me going on to college after high school?' Her answer was always the same: 'That would be wonderful, but I think you may have to earn a scholarship.' Back in those days, money was scarce, as was obtaining financial aid for college. So we all knew that without a scholarship, a college education would have been unattainable for me. This would continue to be a motivating factor throughout my adolescence.

The summer before I was to enter high school, our baseball team from the projects won the summer vacation league for Staten Island. We would represent the borough against the Bronx, Brooklyn, Queens, and Manhattan. We routed Brooklyn, 16-3, and then lost to the Bronx, 6 to 5.

The reward for making it to the Championship Game was that the final two teams got to play an exhibition three-inning game at Yankee Stadium in early September, prior to a Yankees Game. Mind you, it was 1961. The Yankees team that year is today considered to be among the best of all time in baseball. So you could imagine the electricity in the stadium during their pennant race that fall. More importantly, Mickey Mantle and Roger Maris were engulfed in the greatest home run race of all time, as both were hot on the heels of Babe Ruth's home run record of 60 for a season. The night we took the field at Yankee Stadium, I think Maris had 57 home runs, and Mantle had 54.

After we concluded our three-inning game, the Yankees management gave each of us a baseball that we could ask the players to sign during batting practice and warm-ups. So there I was, a kid two days away from entering high school, standing on the steps of the Yankees dugout getting my ball signed by Roger Maris, Yogi Berri, Whitey Ford, Elston Howard, Bobby Richardson, and the rest of the legendary Yankees. Back then, sports memorabilia was not a big thing (or a thing at all, really), but I remember that ball adorning the top of my dresser for the longest time. When the following spring arrived, one of my friends asked, 'Does anyone have a baseball?' Looking to jump into the first choose-up game of the season, of course I yelled back, 'Yes, I have one!' So I ran home, plucked the signed ball from the dresser, and it was used for the first game of the project kids for the spring of 1962! I can only venture a guess as to what that ball signed by most of the '61 Yankees would be worth today, had I kept it in pristine condition! I know, *I know*, but it was a different time. We couldn't exactly shuffle over to the nearest Sporting Goods store and cough up pennies and lint for a new ball, so utilizing a one-of-a-kind professional baseball in a pick-up game back then not only made sense, but was a necessity.

During my years growing up in the South Beach Projects I played on numerous football, baseball and basketball teams. All were well organized and in most cases we were coached by competent role models. By the time I entered high school my foundations in all of these sports was strong and extensive. I was taught the fundamentals of these sports properly, which made the transition to high school sports much easier for me.

As I prepared for the jump into high school sports, I clearly remember feeling that with this transition I would also be representing the South Beach Projects as well as all the other kids I grew up playing and competing with. I also felt a responsibility to the many adults and coaches who had nurtured, advised and guided me during my formative years. I didn't want to let any of them down. Carrying this torch would remain a driving force for me throughout high school and college. I never forgot where I came from, and I always aspired to achieve in hopes of making them all proud of me.

In September of 1961, I headed off to New Dorp High School. From day one, my goal was to make my mark there as an athlete.

New Dorp High School was known as a perennial football powerhouse. In 1959, they had won the New York City Public School Championship, which was televised throughout the Tri-State area. New Dorp HS was led by the legendary coach, Sal Somma; so I was ready not only to play for Coach Somma, but I was convinced that I would naturally be the program's next big star.

The first day of tryouts, the notice on the bulletin board said: 'Football tryouts – report to the men's gymnasium at 3pm'. So at 3pm, I headed for the gym, and what I got was my first dose of reality. The gym was packed with 500 athletes who all had the same idea I had, which was to make the team and become its next big star.

I realized immediately, wow – this was not going to be easy. The competition was going to be fierce, as many of the other kids appeared to be bigger, stronger, and tougher than I was. At the time, I was 5' 10" and maybe 160 pounds. But I was fast, could throw, catch, and knew the game well, having learned the fundamentals in the preceding years as I'd played and had been coached in the Pop Warner Leagues.

Nevertheless, I had some serious soul searching to do. *How am I going to do this? Am I good enough? What do I have to do to get an edge on the competition?*

Back in those days, New Dorp HS was on a double session: freshman attended during the late-session, which meant starting at 11:30am and finishing around 5:15pm. So the first thing I decided to do to create my edge was to get up early each day, put on my workout clothes, then head for the playground and work out. I did sprints, push-ups, sit-ups, stretching, and anything else I could do each day to fine tune my body and skills.

By my sophomore year, I had made the Junior Varsity, but ended up missing some games because I'd forgotten that academics were equally as important as athletics. Once I applied myself both academically and athletically, I was golden. As a sophomore, what I realized most was that I was playing with an extremely smart and talented group. The team had all the pieces to be great and to accomplish special things.

At the beginning of my junior year, I was one of the starting halfbacks in a backfield that consisted of Jimmy Fagan, the other halfback, fullback Walter Mashlykin and quarterback Luke Sherlock. All of them were touted as bona fide all-city prospects, and all were extremely talented. I was honored and thrilled to be part of this gifted backfield. Our coach, Sal Somma, was in his prime and coached us with the passion of a coach who knew he might have a once-in-a-lifetime group.

We were proclaimed to be among the best teams in New Dorp HS Football history, a history that was previously accomplished and heralded.

Our first game in the fall of 1963 was against John Adams HS from Queens, NY. They were a veteran squad and also had championship visions. We lost that first game 12-7, and it was nothing short of heartbreaking. The agony of that loss ran deep in each of us, especially since our reputation, now on the line, had set us out to be the best ever.

Our tragic defeat must have taught us many lessons because we never lost again. We won our remaining seven games that season, convincingly.

As we prepared for our senior year, we were picked as a pre-season favorite to win the city's PSAL (Public School Athletic League) Championship. We began the 1965 season with a big win over Bayside HS in Queens. Seven more convincing wins would follow, culminating with a 26-18 triumph over DeWitt Clinton HS of the Bronx, in the City Championship Game. We finished the 1965 magical season undefeated, 8-0. Myself and Jimmy Fagan were dubbed the 'Touch Down Twins' by the *New York Daily News*, and both of us were selected to the NYC All-City Team - quite an honor - and I won the city scoring championship, tallying 102 points in our eight games.

Today, the 1965 football squad is considered the best football team in New Dorp HS Football history.

In the summers, I played a lot of baseball. Staten Island has a rich history of being a notoriously baseball-obsessed town. It was not uncommon during baseball season to play five or six organized games per week in various leagues such as The Babe Ruth League, The Police Athletic League, and the American Legion League. All were well run and competitive.

My favorite was the American Legion League and I played for the Huttner Pasqualini Post. The summer after my junior year in high school, we won the Staten Island Championship and went on to defeat the Brooklyn and Bronx teams, which entitled us to represent New York City in the statewide American Legion Tournament held in Cooperstown, New York. Cooperstown is the home of the Baseball Hall of Fame and a beautiful little hamlet.

We made it to the Championship Game in 1964. The game was scheduled to start at 3pm. After having breakfast the coaches reminded us to be at Abner Doubleday Field by 1:30pm, which gave us a few hours to do some sightseeing. Cooperstown is bordered by a large and beautiful lake. As we headed down to it, we came upon a marina and noticed that speed boat rentals were available. We ended up renting four boats for an hour, four players to each boat. After about twenty minutes of cruising around the lake, we must have become bored and started playing chicken with each other. By chicken, I mean each boat would come close to the other, narrowly missing one another.

Eventually, we started to bump into each other's boats. At the time we thought that this was hilarious. However, when our hour was up and we headed back to the marina, approaching the dock, we noticed a couple of State Police vehicles with their emergency lights flashing standing alongside our coaches at the end of the dock. Turns out we had forgotten to practice boat safety during our time on the lake - and I don't just mean forgetting to strap on life vests. Additionally, our immature behavior had caused some damage to the boats. Not only did we get a serious reprimand from the coaches, but our actions cost the coaches and our parents around two thousand dollars to cover the damage we had caused to the boats. To say that we were in the doghouse would be a serious understatement. Reflecting back, it was a stupid thing we all participated in, and we were lucky that no one was hurt. We all felt extremely bad over the incident, and all of us wished we had shown better judgment.

Now it was time to get ready for the Championship Game, which, in retrospect, we were lucky to be competing in, as an alternative result to our exciting foray on the waters could have been an afternoon (or more) behind bars instead.

The New York State Championship Game started at 3pm sharp. We must have taken our frustration, or should I say embarrassment, out on the other team. We won the game 18-0, which entitled us to move on to the Eastern Regional tournament to be held at the University of Maryland. The following week, we played teams from Washington D.C., Philadelphia, and Baltimore. Once again, we were victorious. Now it was on to the American Legion World Series, held in Little Rock, Arkansas.

Thanks to American Legion baseball, I got to experience my first airplane flight, as we headed off to Little Rock. Although, sadly, we didn't win the World Series, we did get to compete against teams from Los Angeles, Detroit, and Dallas. It was quite a summer, and when we returned to Staten Island, we did so as conquering heroes. We all headed back to school in the fall, extremely proud of the new heights we had reached.

Chapter 3
Am I Really Going To College?

In the fall of 1965, I was off to college, after being recruited and offered a football scholarship to perennial Division III football powerhouse Missouri Valley College. After accepting the scholarship, it proudly dawned on me that I would be the first person in my family to attend college.

When I arrived in Marshall, Missouri, a town of approximately 16,000 residents, located 80 miles east of Kansas City and ten miles north of Interstate 70, I immediately realized that, once again, I was stepping up to advanced competition, just like when I first walked into the gym for tryouts as a freshman at New Dorp High School.

Once on campus, I was assigned a roommate. His name was Tom Kurucz, and he was from Cheektowaga, NY, which I later learned was located just outside of Buffalo. Tom was a cross between Arnold Schwarzenegger and Vin Diesel. He was 6'3" tall weighed about 225 pounds, and was all muscle from head to toe. Now, at this point, I had grown to 5"11" and weighed about 172 pounds myself. Not that I wasn't proud of the progress I had already made with my physique, but the thought immediately occurred to me that I might consider bulking up a bit before I drowned in the sea of brawn out there! So much of my freshman year was spent learning the system and getting bigger, stronger, and faster. I began eating much more than I had been used to, and then started lifting weights. By the time I returned home for Christmas break that year, I had gained several pounds of muscle and weighed in at 185 pounds. I was ready!

I was a starting tailback from my sophomore year through my senior year and had a wonderful college football career at Missouri Valley College. One of the highlights of playing football at Missouri Valley was having the opportunity to travel through the Midwest. We played in Kansas, Texas, Nebraska, Iowa, Illinois, South Dakota, New Mexico, and I'm sure other states that are now eluding me. What an education it was for a young man from Staten Island, New York, to have the opportunity to travel through the Midwest while making new friends and learning about their lifestyles and traditions.

I also played college baseball at Missouri Valley. Every spring, we would travel south and play at a different college each day, all in preparation for our regular season, which would begin later in April. We would travel by bus as far south as Florida and then work our way back to Missouri.

On April 4th, 1968 our bus pulled off the highway in Memphis, Tennessee and headed for a Holiday Inn restaurant on the outskirts of town to feed the fifteen to twenty edacious players. While we were having our meal we noticed numerous emergency vehicles racing past the Holiday Inn with their lights flashing and sirens blaring. At first, we all thought they were responding to a fire or serious car accident.

In the corner of the restaurant, there was a small black and white television. All of a sudden 'Breaking News' appeared boldly on the screen, followed by a reporter informing us that the Rev. Martin Luther King Jr. had been fatally shot at the Lorraine Motel, which was just blocks away from where we were dining.

As best I can remember, we finished up at the restaurant, got back on the bus and headed south on the highway for our next scheduled game. I think about that day often. Ironically, I've only been in Memphis for approximately two hours in my entire life. Unfortunately, it just happened to be at the same time as Martin Luther King Jr. was assassinated just blocks away.

By the time our trip headed back to Missouri a few days later, the country was in chaos. There was rioting in Kansas City, St. Louis, Detroit, Newark and in many other cities throughout the nation. In many respects, the country would never be the same.

Later that year Robert F. Kennedy was assassinated at the Ambassador Hotel in Los Angeles on June 5th, 1968, just two months after the King assassination. I was finishing up my junior year at the time and remember thinking how I was not ready or eager to enter the real world with all the turmoil around us. It was a dangerous, crazy and depressing time, not only in my life but also in our country's history.

Today, when I reflect back on my college experience, I remember sitting in the college auditorium during the first week of my freshman year at Missouri Valley College. It was an orientation. I remember the speaker on stage as being very stern and serious. He opened up his presentation by saying: 'Look to your left; look to your right; of the three of you only one will be here four years from now.' I remember that as if it were yesterday. I also remember thinking, *Well, I'm definitely going to be the remaining one, no doubt about it.* I think the driving force behind this determination was that I couldn't even fathom the thought of not making it to graduation, mainly because if I failed it would have broken my mother's heart. She was so proud that I had become the first person in our family to attend college and wanted so badly for me to have the opportunities that a college degree could potentially afford me. Later on, another speaker got up and said: 'You're all here to earn degrees, so I'm sure all of you know what different degrees stand for.' He went on to say: 'A BS degree stands for Bull Shit, an MS degree More Shit, and a Ph.D. simply stands for Piled Higher and Deeper.' Almost everyone, including me, thought that was quite funny. Interestingly, today I hold all three of those degrees and, considering where I came from, there's nothing shitty about any of them. Instead, I feel a great deal of gratitude, especially in making my mom proud.

At the conclusion of my football career at Missouri Valley College, Head Coach Ken Gibler handed me a letter that was addressed to me. I immediately noticed that it was from the Washington Redskins. I quickly opened the envelope with the

Redskins bright red logo in the left hand corner. It was a beautifully written letter from Coach Vince Lombardi inviting me to their tryout camp to be held in Washington D.C. that June. Mr. Lombardi was entering his first year as head coach of the Redskins after a legendary career with the Green Bay Packers.

At the time I was already enrolled in graduate school, and now I would have to give Mr. Lombardi's invitation some serious thought and consideration. My first concern was that I had just survived four years of high school football and four years of college football without getting any serious injuries. I felt fortunate and a bit lucky about this. To continue this good fortune in professional football was a serious consideration. Secondly, back in 1970 professional football players DID NOT make the kind of money afforded to the players of today. In fact, most professional players worked at side jobs during the off season to make ends meet. Therefore, the monetary aspect of playing professional football was not much of an incentive back then. Most played simply because they loved the game.

After much soul searching I decided to pass on Coach Lombardi's invitation, and instead continue my education in graduate school. I proceeded to write Coach Lombardi a letter thanking him for his invitation to attend the Washington Redskins Camp and explaining my decision to continue my education instead.

I cherished Coach Lombardi's letter for years. Unfortunately, during one of my home moves the letter was lost. I regret not taking better care of that letter from one of the greatest coaches in NFL history. If I had, today it would be framed and placed on the wall next to me in my office.

I graduated in May of 1969 with a Bachelor of Science Degree. Mom and Dad, along with my brother Mark, drove all the way from Staten Island, New York to Marshall, Missouri to attend the graduation ceremony. I had become the first person in my family to graduate from college, and the sense of pride and accomplishment I felt was overwhelming.

That summer I decided to continue my education and enrolled in the graduate program at Central Missouri State

University, which was located fifty miles east of Kansas City and roughly twenty-five miles southwest of the Missouri Valley College campus where I had spent the previous four years. Central Missouri State was located in Warrensburg, Missouri and it was a real College Town. By that I mean Warrensburg had approximately 14,000 residents and Central Missouri State had over 15,000 students. Everything in Warrensburg revolved around the College.

On a beautiful June afternoon I arrived on campus to enroll for graduate classes. I was quickly informed that all of the on-campus housing was full. Undergraduate students had priority. To solve the housing issue someone mentioned that there was a trailer park eight miles from campus that was renting trailers to students. So off I went to the little town of Knob Noster, Missouri which had a population of approximately 2,000 residents. My father called it a one-horse town. Knob Noster is located adjacent to Whiteman Air Force Base, which is known for being a vital part of the Air Force Global Strike Command, which makes sense being located in the geographic center of the United States. The sound of high tech bombers landing and taking off was an everyday occurrence.

I ended up renting a trailer in Knob Noster for the year I attended graduate school. It's a good thing my 1962 Thunderbird held up for the eight mile trip to and from campus each day, because public transportation was non-existent.

When I reflect back on my year living in a trailer park, the one factor that never came to mind was safety. Missouri is right in the heart of tornado alley and the last place you want to be should a tornado strike is in a trailer. It's the number one most dangerous environment to be in during a tornado. Back then, I didn't even have a plan of where to take shelter when a tornado warning was issued.

To illustrate how dangerous tornadoes can be, on May of 2011 in Joplin, Missouri, which is located 100 miles south of Knob Noster and my old trailer park, was devastated by an EF5 rated multiple-vortex tornado. The tornado's mile path cut right through the southern part of the city killing 156 people, and injuring 1,150 others. The Joplin tornado ranks as the costliest in United States history; insurance payouts exceeded $2.8 billion.

When I think back, I'm not sure why I wasn't more aware and prudent regarding the dangers of living in a trailer in the heart of tornado alley. At the very least I should have had a take cover plan during warnings. However, when you're in your 20s you think you're invincible; in my case I think I was just stupid, careless and lucky. Never having to deal with anything as ferocious as the Joplin tornado was just good fortune.

In August of 1970, I completed my graduate school studies at Central Missouri State University. Having earned my Master of Science degree I decided to head back home to New York City and attempt to enter the job market.

Forty years had passed before I returned to Missouri Valley College in 2012 to serve as the commencement speaker at graduation. When I was originally asked to serve as the keynote speaker at graduation in 2012, I called current Missouri Valley College President Dr. Bonnie Humphrey for some advice on giving my speech. She laughed, and said: 'You're a rock star! Just prepare something compelling for about 20 minutes and you'll be fine.' She then finished our conversation by saying with a giggle: 'I hope no one ever asks me to serve as a commencement speaker.' Right then I knew I had a tremendous task ahead of me - write a 20-minute speech that was compelling and interesting, with a tasteful touch of humor.

I worked on that speech for three months, fine-tuning, timing and fine-tuning again.

The big day arrived, and I would be delivering the commencement address on the football field with thousands in attendance sitting in the stands. The graduation ceremony began at high noon, and on this day it was 96°, hot and humid. As I awaited my introduction to step up to the podium and give my address, I could feel the sweat running down my chest under my cap and gown.

Before my introduction, several people needed to be escorted to the First Aid Station after being overcome by the heat. Watching this, I leaned over to President Humphrey and expressed my concern, 'What if I succumb to the heat?' She chuckled and said, 'If that happens, try and leave your notes on the podium and I'll finish your speech.'

Thankfully, that didn't happen and my commencement address went off even better than I had hoped it would. Because I had worked so hard on the speech, I was totally prepared for the experience. I will always remember it as a highlight of my life.

One of the points I emphasized during my address to the graduating class was 'in the pursuit of your dream, you're likely to receive many "No's" along the way, as I did. But keep reminding yourself that all you need is one "Yes" to move forward on your dream.'

I also mentioned a recent *Profiles* interview I had conducted with Billy Blanks, the creator of the 'Tae Bo' fitness program. Billy was diagnosed with Attention Deficit Disorder in high school and was placed in Special Education classes. Yet he became extremely successful in business, selling over 100 million exercise videos in 32 different languages.

During our interview Billy said something really interesting when he said, 'The more successful you become, the more obstacles you'll experience.' He went on to say, 'Less successful, fewer obstacles.' Many feel it would be just the opposite. Billy went on to say that he felt the key to his success was expecting obstacles and having a detour plan for each obstacle he faced. He then said that 'most people and businesses do not have a detour plan when disaster strikes, and are usually caught by surprise.'

I did my research, and I think Billy is right. I reviewed the Dow Jones Industrial Index when it was first established over 100 years ago. Astonishingly, only one company still survives from that original index – General Electric. Why did 99 of the original companies fail?

Financial experts claim it was a combination of things that include the lack of an adequate detour plan in the face of adversity, as Billy said, along with growing competitiveness around the world, and rapid changes in technology. Most importantly, these failures underscore the importance of reinvention in the face of a global economy.

No company is a better example of this than Eastman Kodak. If you're old enough, you know what a 'Kodak Moment' is. Kodak is a 138-year-old company, and at one time one of the strongest brands in the world. Here are some facts: Kodak was founded in 1880 by high school dropout George Eastman in Rochester, New York. Almost a century later, in 1969, Neil Armstrong used a Kodak camera to take pictures on the moon. Nearly every movie that's won Best Picture at the Oscars was shot on Kodak film. Kodak was a pioneer of digital photography, yet failed to protect and adapt to the new era it helped to create. Since 2003, Kodak has closed over 140 plants and laid off approximately 47,000 employees. Ultimately, the company failed to diversify, had inadequate detour plans, and filed for bankruptcy in 2012.

Of the 100 original companies on the Dow Jones Industrial Index there are 99 similar stories. According to Billy Blanks, much can be learned from all of this, such as: 'Expect obstacles in life and business and always have a backup plan. Always be open to reinvention, don't be afraid to change. Know your history; it does have a tendency to repeat itself. And most importantly, never get caught up in the "culture of complacency." '

During my commencement address I shared the following message: 'I've been on television in New York City for the past 25 years, so I can tell you, fame is not all that it's cracked up to be. Yet the desire to be famous in this country, with or without talent, is all around us. All you have to do is sit and watch an evening of reality programs.'

I went on to say: 'So, what's really important? This is what Dr. Martin Luther King said: "Not everybody can be famous. But everybody can be great, because greatness is determined by service." ' I then told the students: 'No matter what you do on your journey from here today, don't forget to give back. Give back to your community, give back to your family, and give back to your school.'

I finished up by reading a quote from legendary UCLA Basketball Coach John Wooden who once wrote: 'You can't live a perfect day without doing something for someone who will never be able to repay you.'

After my address, President Humphrey presented me with an honorary Doctorate in Philosophy, in front of the thousands in attendance. I was one proud puppy!

These days, President Humphrey and her staff visit New York City to have dinner with alumni once or twice a year. At one of the first dinners, President Humphrey noticed that I was wearing my college ring and said: 'I can't believe you're still wearing your college ring, did you put it on just for me today?' Without hesitation, I looked her straight in the eye and responded: 'I've worn this ring every day since my senior year at Missouri Valley College, it represents what attaining a college degree means to me and how that experience changed my life forever.'

Chapter 4
Time To Get A Job

After graduating from Missouri Valley College in May of 1969, I immediately enrolled in the graduate program at Central Missouri State University in Warrensburg, Missouri about 20 miles southeast of Marshall. In August of 1970, I had earned my Master's degree and headed back to Staten Island with one thing on my mind: it's time to get serious and get a job.

My heart wanted me to go into broadcasting, but my head told me to go into teaching and coaching. Since this was B.C. (Before Cable) and opportunities in media were extremely limited, the choice was clear, and I found myself returning to my old high school.

I began my first job as an Assistant Football Coach to the legendary Sal Somma at New Dorp High School. He was a coaching master, and I had the honor of learning everything I know about coaching from him. I absorbed everything I could from Mr. Somma, first as a player of his and now as an assistant coach. I think I learned something new from him every day I had the honor of being in his presence. I loved his repetitive system, the discipline he taught, and most importantly, the way he treated his players. He treated everyone with respect, and I don't think I ever heard him use profanity. But make no mistake, he WAS the BOSS and he earned the ultimate respect from everyone.

In 1973, I was transferred as a teacher to McKee High School on the North Shore of Staten Island, a stone's throw from the famous Staten Island Ferry. Once at McKee, I met athletic director Bob Steele, who was looking for a junior varsity basketball coach and offered me the job. I accepted. Basketball was the last sport I had envisioned myself coaching. I felt I was better equipped to coach football or baseball. But here I was, the Head Junior Varsity Basketball Coach at McKee High School.

What I decided to do right from the start was to take everything I had learned about coaching from Sal Somma and apply it to basketball. I incorporated his practice routines, team discipline, and repetition techniques during practice. I was applying the Sal Somma Football Coaching Philosophy to a completely different sport, but it worked like a charm.

As a football player at New Dorp High School, we had won the New York City Public School Athletic League Championship in the 1964 season, with an undefeated record of 8 and 0. Now, as a basketball coach at Mckee High School on Staten Island, I wondered if I could be as equally successful.

My first group of players at McKee were a talented group. However, the first year was spent incorporating discipline while getting the kids to buy into my system, which was a more disciplined system than most of them had been used to playing.

This first group consisted of Steve Robinson, a talented and gifted point guard; Darrell Cress, a great shooting guard; his brother Wade Cress, who I used as a swingman, although he could play inside or outside; and Demetrius Means, or 'D' as we all called him, who at 6 foot 3 inches, I used as a center. D was the heart and soul of the group that I would coach over the next four years. The kid was a talented player, but more importantly, he oozed with personality, and his leadership skills were the kind that every coach aspires to have on their team. Over the years, Demetrius and I have remained close friends. I don't think he's ever missed calling me on my birthday since he left high school ages ago.

So right out of the box, I had this talented and smart group in front of me. I knew immediately that they were a special group, and interestingly, so did they. The challenge was to teach them discipline, which I knew was not going to be an easy task. Most of them were stars in the middle school level and playground leagues growing up. They were successful using their talent and doing their own thing. That was about to change. I was going to incorporate a system that required discipline from each and every player. At first, some players were reluctant to try it. It took time and patience. People in general hate change and my first group was no different. However, once they realized that my disciplined system was non-negotiable, little by little, things began to fall into place.

We worked through wrinkles, enough to win the PSAL Junior Varsity Championship on Staten Island that first year. The next year, a transfer student from North Carolina walked through the door and forever changed the game for us. Kenny Page was a sophomore, and he was a great shooter. He was the missing link the team we already had needed. Now, with Kenny, we could be truly great. Athletic Director Bob Steele decided to keep the group together and continue on the junior varsity level for one more year. The result was an undefeated season, twenty wins and no losses in 1974-1975.

The next year, I became the Varsity Coach; it was time to play with the big boys, the varsity. After a slow start, we ended up going 17-4 while losing in the first round of the citywide championships.

By the time the group became seniors, they were rated number one in many pre-season polls. No Staten Island high school basketball team had ever won a Public School City Championship, so many wondered if this McKee team be the first.

My team was now mature, experienced and polished. We were entering the final year of a four-year project, and the anticipation was enormous. Everything went as planned in that 1977-78 season as we reeled off win after win, and finished the regular season 20 wins and no losses while being rated in the top 20 nationwide.

We entered the citywide playoffs as one of the favorites to win it all. We cruised through the first three playoff games, making it to the finals.

In the finals, we would be facing Dewitt Clinton High School of the Bronx, a perennial powerhouse. It's worth mentioning that McKee had nine hundred boys attending, whereas Dewitt Clinton had closer to six thousand. It was truly a David and Goliath scenario.

The championship game was played at St. John's University in the spring of 1978. The game was tied at halftime 36-36. In the second half, their size wore us down a bit and we ended up losing 72-66. We finished that season 23-1. To this day, that McKee team is the only public high school team from Staten Island ever to make it to the city championship game.

In the late 70s CBS premiered a television series starring Ken Howard called *The White Shadow*. In the series Howard took a job coaching at an impoverished urban high school with a racially mixed basketball team; however, most of his players were predominantly black. The series in many respects mirrored our team at McKee High School, and we were often reminded of the similarities. Racism was one topic that often surfaced on the TV series. Unfortunately, at times I also witnessed and had to deal with various forms of racism from fans, parents and adults of opposing teams, and from places you might least expect it. One day I was called down to the Principal's office. I thought I was being summoned to receive some form of congratulations for the completion of an undefeated season, which I did receive initially. Then, to my dismay the Principal said to me: 'Why don't you take some more white players on your team?' I immediately replied: 'I don't select players on our team based on the color of their skin, but rather I choose them on their talent, character, potential and work ethic. I couldn't care less if they are white, black or green.' Some things never cease to amaze me; that was a great example of one of those times.

I ended up coaching at McKee High School for thirteen seasons, which included a couple more undefeated seasons and Staten Island Championships. However, when I reflect back today, what I'm most proud of are not the unblemished seasons or championships, but rather, the long term success of the kids I coached; that's what is closest to my heart. I can't think of one example of any of my players over those thirteen seasons and beyond getting into trouble, getting arrested, or doing anything to embarrass themselves or their families.

Today, many of my former players have gone on to become teachers, pastors, social workers, hotel managers, broadcasters and military leaders. Whatever the reasons for the long term good fortunes of my former players, I'm not entirely sure. However, the fact is, the success and happiness of the kids I coached is without a doubt what I'm most proud of when I reflect back on my coaching career. I retired from coaching in 1988.

Aside from teaching and coaching, I also had a love of singing and performing, and for a period of time in the late 1970s, twice a week I would take the Staten Island Ferry into Manhattan, then take the subway to the Upper Westside for vocal lessons with professional voice coach Bill Shepard. My goal was to improve my vocal skills to the point that I would have the confidence to form my own band, something I had always wanted to do.

One of my best friends, Jimmy Scara, was an accomplished saxophone player and songwriter. In 1979, Jimmy wrote a ballad called 'You're The Reason', for which I wrote the lyrics. Jimmy encouraged me to provide the lead vocals and I enthusiastically agreed. Jimmy rounded up his musician friends and our first band was formed; it would be called Mickey Burns and Company. In late 1979, we went into the recording studio and recorded 'You're The Reason' as the A-side, and 'Think I'm In Love Again' as the B-side. Back in the late 70s, 45rpm vinyl records were still the way you purchased and listened to your favorite songs. We had a few thousand copies of our record pressed into 45s and gave them out everywhere. We were very proud of our record, and the feedback from those who listened to it was consistently positive.

The plan at that point was to approach every record label in New York City in hopes of getting signed, which would provide proper distribution and management for our record. Although many said they liked it, eventually they all passed.

Not to be deterred, the band decided to keep moving forward. As Jimmy continued working on new material, the band got booked in numerous cabaret nightclubs in Manhattan and throughout New York City. In 1980, we added Dave Fitzgerald to the band as lead guitarist and Donna Tucker as the female vocalist. Donna was a cross between Whitney Houston and Donna Summer; she was beautiful and her voice was spectacular. Most importantly, audiences loved her.

As the band got tighter, we continued to perform in clubs all over the city. My favorite was Dangerfield's, owned by legendary comedian Rodney Dangerfield. Back in the early 80s, each night, Dangerfield's featured a comedy act, followed by a musical act. Rodney himself would perform there often, mostly to test out new material. As the musical act, we would perform two shows, one at 10pm followed by a second show at 1am. The audiences at Dangerfield's were great and came from all over the country. They were mostly tourists visiting New York City, and they were attentive and wanted to be entertained.

Reflecting back, we didn't make much money at Dangerfield's, maybe fifty dollars for each member per night. However, it was a great place to showcase our band. One night after our first show I was approached by a young couple from Long Island. They both expressed how much they loved our band and said they were getting married in six months and wanted to know if we would consider playing at their wedding. We were not a wedding band, we were a show band looking for a record deal. However, I told them the band would discuss it and that I would get back to them in about a week.

Later that night I told the band about the offer. At first, most of the band members were resistant and replied, 'We're not a wedding band.' I agreed, but I told all of them to let me do some research and find out exactly what it was that a wedding band needed to know and do, and we would then discuss it again.

What I quickly learned was that wedding bands made a lot of money compared to playing in clubs and cabarets. At the time wedding bands were earning from two thousand to five thousand dollars per wedding, depending on the band's popularity and experience. Additionally, the hours were better. For example, many weddings are held from 7pm to 11pm, a far better scenario than heading home from a club at 3am. Another big difference was that as a show band, we played the music we loved and created, whereas as a wedding band, we would need to know how to play everything, and that included Motown, disco, swing, standards, top 40, the 60s, 70s, 80s, etc. and just about every ethnic song. For example, if we were playing a Jewish wedding, 'Hava Nagila' would be at the top of our lineup; and if it was an Italian wedding, we'd better be ready to pour our hearts into 'The Tarantella', and maybe even throw some footwork in there ourselves.

After all the research was done, I shared it with the band and we decided to accept that first wedding from the couple on Long Island. It turned out great, and all the band members more than liked the experience - and the raise in pay was more than welcome.

From there, I hooked up with a few booking agencies for wedding bands in the Tri-state area. Before long we started booking numerous weddings while increasing our repertoire to accommodate any wedding. We filled our calendar by performing at what is known as 'wedding showcases' in New York and New Jersey. At wedding showcases, we would perform a fifteen minute set in front of twenty to thirty engaged couples in attendance who were there to book the band of their liking for their upcoming wedding. Usually, a showcase would feature three to four bands. At the end of the evening, the couples would select and book the band they liked the most for their wedding.

By the mid-1980s we had become a full-fledged wedding band. We started out doing twenty weddings a year, then forty weddings a year. By 1989, we had evolved into one of the more popular wedding bands in the New York Tri-State area. That year, we performed at over a hundred weddings. Our weekends were jammed: a gig on Friday night, two on Saturdays, and two on Sundays. We were at a grueling pace.

The one thing that set us apart from the other bands at the showcases was that we didn't just get up and perform songs like our competition: we put on a show, costumes and all. I would always start off with my best Tom Jones, tight pants and open shirt, singing 'Delilah'. Our female vocalist Donna then came out and performed a dead-on Whitney Houston. She would follow that up with either Donna Summer or Diana Ross. Donna had all of them down perfectly, both looks and vocals. For the finale, I would finish up by performing an Elvis medley, jumpsuit and all. Our audiences loved it! It must have been difficult for many of the other bands to compete against. Ultimately, the number of dates our band was booking validated that what we were doing was hitting a chord with the couples at the showcases.

I left the music business in the early 1990s for two reasons. First, Disc Jockeys were beginning to become popular at weddings, mainly because they were far less expensive than bands. Therefore, it became increasingly difficult to fill our calendar as we had been doing for many years. Additionally, I was getting tired of the hectic schedule of performances, showcases, and rehearsals. Also, I was starting to freelance at Fox News in New York City as a sound man on the news crews. I had always aspired to a career in broadcasting, and now that I had my foot in the door, I wanted to take full advantage of this opportunity.

Once I got a taste of the broadcasting industry, I was hooked. It was everything I'd hoped it would be, and I loved it from day one. Over the next twenty-five years, broadcasting would become a major part of my life. I would go on to do pretty much everything in the business: producing, writing, reporting, interviewing, hosting - you name it. When I reflect back that I've been on the air in the number one television market in the world every week for the past twenty years, doing what I love, what I feel is an enormous amount of gratitude.

Chapter 5
Finally Getting Into Broadcasting

During college, I had a strong interest in pursuing a broadcasting career. I thought becoming a sports journalist might be the perfect path for me. After all, my love of sports ran deep and I was pretty knowledgeable about all sports.

However, I was also realistic and at the time I noticed that most of those who did the sports on the 6pm and 11pm newscasts were former professional athletes. The late 60s was a time in television that I call B.C., before cable. I'm sure many will remember that back then, there was only CBS, NBC, ABC and a couple of local channels. I also knew that if I was going to pursue a broadcasting career it was highly unlikely that I would have an opportunity to start in New York City, the media capital of the world. More than likely, my start would have taken a more traditional path like: first step, Biloxi, Mississippi, then on to Boise, Idaho, and then if I got really good I could have possibly worked my way into a bigger market like Columbus, Ohio. In broadcasting, only the cream of the crop make it to New York City, a fact that I was well aware of; but I was eager to get back there, to my roots and my home. So rather than take what would have been an extremely challenging path in broadcasting, I decided to come home to New York City and begin teaching and coaching.

In the late 80s, I finally got into the broadcasting industry, but entirely by accident. My best friend Richie Murphy was a cameraman at Fox Television for over 30 years. On the weekends we would play golf together. He would also recruit some of his colleagues at Fox to frequently join us. They included then anchors Bill McCreary and John Roland, and medical reporter Max Gomez, among others. Many of them were considered celebrities, and because of them, whatever course we were playing, we were treated like royalty.

I would become friends with many of the reporters and anchors at Fox in New York City. In fact, Bill McCreary would become my mentor when I eventually made the jump into broadcasting.

One day while we were playing golf, my friend Richie Murphy said to me: 'My partner at Fox is going on vacation, do you want me to see if you could replace him as a sound man for the 10 o'clock news until he returns?' I answered, 'Yes, that would be great, sounds like fun.' I had extensive knowledge of sound equipment through my many years of playing in bands and thought this transition would be an easy one.

My first day at Fox, with Richie as a cameraman and myself handling sound, we were joined by reporter Pablo Guzman and headed down to City Hall to cover a press conference. After that, we were told to head uptown to Yankee Stadium and get some sound bites from players on the field during batting practice.

When we returned to the Fox headquarters on 67th Street, I was immediately asked if I could work the rest of the week. I gracefully accepted.

After working at Fox for about six months I got a call from Richie who said, 'I got you on a special I'll be doing, it has something to do with domestic violence, you'll handle the sound on the remote shoots.' I was thrilled to be getting the work, and working with one of my best friends was always fun.

Richie told me to be at the station by 6pm on Saturday night. He explained that we would leave from there and then head out to the police station in Plainfield, New Jersey. The plan was to hang out at the police station until a domestic violence call came in and then accompany the police to the location of the incident. Our goal was to document everything on video.

We headed out of the city through the Lincoln Tunnel and arrived at the Plainfield Police Headquarters around 7pm. I remember thinking we might be sitting in the station all night if a domestic violence call didn't come in. That fear was short lived. Literally five minutes after we arrived a police sergeant approached us and said, 'You're on, we just got a call from a woman several blocks away who said her husband was beating her, let's go.' On the way out of the station the sergeant turned to us and said, 'The women also said he's got a knife, things could turn violent so stay on your toes.' As Richie and I sat in the back of the squad car we both started getting a bit nervous, not knowing what to expect.

In roughly five minutes we pulled up to the house of the woman who had made the call. Immediately she came running out of the house screaming, 'He's in the house out of control and he's carrying a knife!' The police opened the trunk and quickly put on their bullet proof vests while saying to us, 'Stay close behind, let's go.' I then whispered to Richie, 'Do you think we should be wearing bullet proof vests as well?' Richie smirked and said, 'Just be careful and stay right behind me."

As we entered the house, which was big and old, sort of like the house in *The Munsters* television series, the first thing we noticed was that it was totally dark - there wasn't a light on in the entire house. The only light was from the flashlights carried by the two police officers in front of us.

After canvassing the first floor unsuccessfully we headed up a narrow stairway leading to the second floor. At the top of the stairs one of the officers noticed a window half opened and said, 'I think the guy may have jumped out here, let's go back down and check out the backyard.' As we circled around the house to the backyard it was equally as dark; the only light was provided by the police officers' flashlights.

The backyard was full of bushes, hedges, and ankle deep fallen leaves. As the police were searching within the hedges with their flashlights I was looking back at the house. All of a sudden I thought I noticed the tip of a sneaker barely hanging over the ledge on the second floor. I leaned over to Richie and asked him to turn on his camera light and direct it towards the second floor ledge. As he began scanning the ledge with his light we quickly realized the guy we were looking for was hiding right in front of us on the dark second floor ledge.

From behind us I could hear one of the police officers yelling, 'There he is!' Realizing that he was spotted, the man on the ledge stood up erect as the officers started running towards the building. Shockingly, the man on the ledge, doing his best version of Spider-Man, leaped off the second floor ledge onto the police officers below. After a brief struggle rolling around on the ground, the police officers were able to handcuff the man and get him under control.

As the man was being escorted to the police vehicle I leaned over to Richie and said, 'Can you believe what just happened? And we documented every second of the entire incident.' The domestic violence special ended up winning an Emmy Award for Fox. Richie later told me that the footage we captured that night became the inspiration for the hit series *Cops* which remained on the air for years. I'll never forget that night in Plainfield, New Jersey. It remains etched in my memory forever.

I enjoyed my time as part of the news crews at Fox News in New York City. I always felt that the crews never got the credit they deserved for capturing the news out in the field each and every day. It's a tough job, and back in the 1980s the equipment was heavy and the weather was irrelevant - snow, rain, hot or cold, the crews were in it, and getting the story was all that mattered.

When covering breaking news, it was high pressure. We had to get to the location quickly, many times through heavy Manhattan traffic. Once there, we had to jockey to get the best spot available to capture the story. In many instances, we were fighting for space among the other ten to fifteen news crews at the location, there to get the same story. Everyone tried to cooperate, but sometimes it was a difficult task.

In the summer of 1989, our crew spent weeks outside of the Federal Courthouse in downtown Manhattan waiting for a verdict to be delivered in the Central Park jogger case. This was a criminal case based on the assault and rape of a 28-year-old white woman jogging in Central Park. The attack was one of the most widely publicized crimes of the 1980s.

Back then, I remember thinking to myself: *When the verdict comes down, we better get everything right; the city and the nation are anxiously awaiting the verdict.* At the end of the trial, all six teenagers were convicted of rape and other charges. The convictions were later appealed and in the second trial it was determined that all six teenagers had been falsely accused and illegally tried in the two trials for the rape. Ultimately, the DNA evidence collected from the scene didn't match up to any of the six teens accused. The teenagers then sued the City of New York for discrimination and emotional distress; the City settled in 2014 for 41 million dollars.

This is how it was for me and the other men and women of the news crew at Fox; you just never knew what was going to happen next. However, what you did know was that when breaking news appeared, you were going to be in the middle of it. It was hard work, but extremely rewarding and exciting.

Right from the start at Fox, my goal was to work myself into an on-air position. So each and every day, I learned as much as I could from the veteran reporters, hosts, and anchors. Every day was an education and I was a sponge.

Then one day, the talk around the newsroom was that Rupert Murdoch was taking over Fox. One of the first things he did was to cut out overtime. Before Rupert arrived, cameramen and editors were making around sixty thousand dollars a year, and most years doubling that salary with overtime. Without overtime, in a matter of a week, many salaries were cut in half, and many wondered how they would make ends meet.

The solution to this problem was to begin moonlighting. So we formed a small group, called Group Four Productions. Our advantage was that we had many connections throughout the broadcasting industry.

Shortly after we formed our moonlighting production company, we were contracted by Time Warner Cable to produce a news magazine, which we called *Special Edition*. We shot stories after-hours and on weekends, and usually edited the stories for air all day Saturday and Sunday evenings. Richie Murphy was the cameraman, Vinnie Russo, the top editor at Fox, was our editor, and Doug Scara did the graphics. Crystal Young was one of our reporters, and I served as the other reporter and host. We had a great team and put together a great news magazine that we were all extremely proud of.

Then one day Richie said to me, 'I think Rupert is giving back overtime, he realizes he can't run an effective news operation without it.'

In essence, what that meant was that our team would no longer have the time to pursue these outside projects. But the experience from Group Four Productions gave me the opportunity to become an on-air talent as a reporter and host. In retrospect, I was always learning from the best, both at Fox and with Group Four Productions.

Shortly after we disbanded and everyone went back to work at Fox, I was hired by Time Warner Cable to host a show called *Staten Island Live*. It was very much like *Larry King Live*. As host and producer, I interviewed local politicians, newsmakers, and the occasional celebrity on the hour-long program.

But more importantly, my broadcasting career was now in full throttle. That was over twenty years ago; I'm still on the air and loving every minute.

While at Fox, I became very close friends with anchor Bill McCreary who also produced his shows *The McCreary Report* and *Black News* at Fox. Everyone loved Bill, and he was, without a doubt, the consummate professional. Bill served as my mentor and coach right from the beginning of my broadcast career, and continues to do so to this day. He taught me how to dress, and how to interview, along with the importance of preparation. He always gave me the unfiltered truth, good and bad. Learning from him has been a blessing and I'm proud to call him my mentor.

I also still play golf with Richie Murphy, who is retired from Fox and spends most of his time in Florida. We played golf together last summer shortly after his 81st birthday; he shot 77 and beat me for ten dollars!

Chapter 6
The Birth of *Profiles*

Moving forward to 1999, my company Quest Media was producing a news magazine called *Special Edition* that was airing on Time Warner. Each episode featured three seven-to-eight-minute segments, one of which was an entertainment segment. Our routine for the entertainment segment was pretty consistent. We would research what celebrities were appearing in various locations around Manhattan, and once we had decided on the celebrity we would be producing a segment on, we would call ahead for press clearance, load the equipment in the car and head for the Staten Island Ferry. Our studio was just minutes away.

This was before 9/11 and cars were allowed on the Staten Island Ferries. It was an absolutely great way to make a trip into the Big Apple. Most nights, we parked our car on the Ferry and even got to take a fifteen to twenty minute nap before departing. Once leaving the ferry, you had a choice of taking the Westside or Eastside highways and depending on the traffic, we usually arrived at our destination within a reasonable time period.

Our goal was to get a 10-minute interview with our selected celebrity of the day. We usually talked about their current and most recent projects.

When we returned to our studios, usually the next day, to begin editing the interview into an air-rebrandable eight-minute segment, I started to realize that many of the celebrities I'd been interviewing went way beyond the eight minutes. In many cases, they wanted to talk about their entire careers, their childhood, and their personal life. Some would talk for twenty minutes, others thirty if time permitted.

My dilemma was having to cut up these great interviews to the required eight minutes maximum, ultimately leaving out a lot of great stuff.

It's painful getting a great interview with a celebrity, only to have more than half of it end up on the cutting room floor. So I decided to create a new thirty-minute talk show and call it *Profiles*.

Why *Profiles*? According to Webster, a profile is defined as a concise overview - and that's exactly what I wanted our new show to be. However, I now had thirty minutes to accomplish that.

Our first attempt at producing a thirty-minute *Profiles* episode came in the summer of 1999 with trumpeter and composer Chuck Mangione. We conducted the interview in the music hall on the grounds of Snug Harbor Cultural Center, where Chuck would be performing that evening. The interview took place at two in the afternoon, prior to Chuck's sound check. The environment was relaxed, and Chuck was more than eager to talk about his life and career.

After the interview I asked Producer Gary Humienny, 'How long was the interview?' He quickly responded, 'Forty minutes.' Although we would have to do some editing down, I knew right there that we had a great episode, a great concept, and an altogether great show moving forward.

In 1999, *Profiles* was only airing exclusively on Time Warner Cable on Staten Island. Yet we were building a large and loyal viewing audience rather quickly. Over the next several months, we produced *Profiles* episodes with some truly great celebrities such as Darlene Love, Pat Cooper, Al Martino, Isaac Hayes, Danny Aiello, Julie Budd, John Amos, Katee Sackhoff, David Johansen, Teddy Atlas and many more. We were on a roll and everyone was buying in, including celebrities who we were reaching out to for appearances on the show.

In 2002, one of our executive producers, Bill McCreary, informed me that then-Mayor Michael R. Bloomberg was getting ready to transform the bare bones operation at the city-run WNYE into a new creative network that would be dubbed as New York City's official network, 'NYC TV'. Bill and I felt immediately that NYC TV would be the perfect fit for the *Profiles* series, in that the series showcased a long line of luminaries who made our great city the entertainment capital of the world.

After months of meetings with the new general manager at NYC TV, Erick Wierson, we were able to work out an agreement and *Profiles* found itself a home on NYC TV.

Profiles made its new premiere in September of 2003. In doing so, we increased our potential viewership to six million. Our first *Profiles* episode on NYC TV featured singer B.J. Thomas, whose unique voice you may recognize from a string of hit singles in the late 1960s and 1970s such as 'Hooked on a Feeling', 'Raindrops Keep Fallin' On My Head' and 'I Just Can't Help Believing', just to mention a few.

By the fall of 2006, we were celebrating our 'One Hundredth Episode Milestone' on NYC TV. In recognition of this accomplishment New York City Mayor Michael R. Bloomberg sent us a beautiful letter that read: 'Over the past three years, your exemplary program has offered a hundred opportunities to learn more about the long line of luminaries who have made our great City the entertainment capital of the world. Congratulations on the success of the One Hundredth Episode Milestone, and I hope *Profiles* continues to educate and inspire us for years to come. Sincerely, Michael R. Bloomberg, Mayor.'

In 2013, NYC TV rebranded itself as NYC Life and we now moved over to channel 25. This move offered our series a tremendous opportunity, in that the potential viewing demographic jumped from six million to eighteen million. *Profiles* could now be seen by pretty much everyone with a television set within a fifty-mile radius of New York City, and that included New Jersey, Long Island, Upstate New York, and Connecticut.

We had worked our way into the number one media market in the world, and our series was smack in the middle of it and continues to be to this day.

A week never goes by when someone doesn't approach me on the street or in the subway to tell me how much they enjoy the show. When this happens I often think of how we're competing with CBS, NBC, CNN and so on, yet through hard work and determination, we've garnered our share of viewership in a competitive television universe. At times, these facts make us feel like the mouse that could, which is perfectly fine with us as we continue to strive to improve with each and every episode.

In October of 2017, we reached our four-hundredth episode, a milestone celebrated by just a handful of television programs in the medium's 70-year history. Our four-hundredth guest was the most famous face in daytime television history, actress Susan Lucci. *TV Guide* recently placed Susan among its Fifty Greatest TV Stars of All-Time. Regarding her appearance on *Profiles*, Lucci said: 'Reminiscing on so many memorable moments of my career with Mickey was great fun! It was an honor to be featured on *Profiles*' four-hundredth episode, a program that has celebrated the careers of so many extraordinary individuals whom I have admired over the years, including the late Dr. Maya Angelou, Smokey Robinson, and LeRoy Neiman. Congratulations to Mickey and the *Profiles* crew on this great milestone.'

Due to the nature of today's television industry, fewer and fewer shows these days seem to be hitting major milestones. This makes our journey to reach episode five hundred even more special and exciting.

Chapter 7
Profiles Top Ten

People often ask me 'Who was your favorite interview?' That's a tough one, especially having interviewed over 450 interesting and, in many cases, famous people. That having been said, here's my attempt at a top ten favorite list (in no specific order).

George Foreman - Former Heavyweight Boxing Champion

Although we talked in-depth about his amazing boxing career - fighting and losing to the great Muhammad Ali, and making a phenomenal comeback in his 40s, in spite of his contemporaries thinking he was much too old and out of shape to do so - what I loved about my interview with George was his business sense. He reminded me that he was a successful pitch man for Midas Mufflers, InventHelp, and of course his own George Foreman Grills, about which he exuberantly stated, 'They really work.'

George said that when the corporate types approached him to use his name on the grill, they asked him what he wanted, to which he responded, 'I have seven sons named George, can I have a grill for each of them?' To this day, I'm still not sure if he was kidding or not. After agreeing to be the front man for the grill, three months later, George said he received a check in the mail for $250,000.

Then George got serious and said, 'The one thing I've learned about business is: a good business deal isn't a good one unless both parties are happy.' That may sound simple, but

George believed that this philosophy was the key to his success in business.

He was more than eager to discuss finding God after a fight in Puerto Rico in 1977. According to George, 'After the fight, I went back to the dressing room and in a split second, I was dead, fighting for my life.' He went on to say, 'I started screaming "Jesus Christ has come alive in me", even though I didn't believe in that stuff.'

The experience impacted George so profoundly that he admits a single day hasn't gone by without him thinking about that day. Prior to his epiphany, George had a lot of hate in his heart: 'My hope was that I was going to kill someone in the ring, then they'd really be afraid of me. I'm going to kill one of these fools. After that experience in Puerto Rico, I couldn't even make a fist for ten years, I couldn't box anymore.'

While reflecting back on his near-death experience, George said: 'The worst thing was, I was about to die and I didn't get to say goodbye to my mother... that bothered me.'

In 1974, George fought the great Muhammad Ali in the 'Rumble in the Jungle'. The fight had captured the interest of sports fans around the world. In his book *God In My Corner* Foreman claims that he was drugged before the fight. George recalls: 'I would always rehydrate just before the fight, but before the Ali fight, the water tasted funny. I'm sure someone put something in it.'

To this day, the fight is known as a classic. Ali won by knockout in round eight. Reflecting back, Foreman explained, 'I was beating him with vicious punches from pillar to post, all the while Ali kept shouting at me "Is that all you have George?" I couldn't believe it!'

Foreman went on to say, 'He finally caught me with that right hand and knocked me out. He was a great champion and beat me fair and square.'

George retired from professional boxing in 1997 at age 48. His final record was 76 wins, 68 of them by knockouts, and 5 losses.

Davy Jones - Former Lead Singer of The Monkees

Davy walked into the interview full of energy, personality and charm off the charts, looking trim and healthy. He quickly reminded me that, way before he became a Monkee, he had been a star on Broadway playing the Artful Dodger in *Oliver*. He also mentioned that in February of 1963, he was on the bill of *The Ed Sullivan Show* to sing a song from the play. When Davy arrived at the Ed Sullivan Theater for the show, he noticed the police barriers that surrounded the theater and thought to himself that they might have been placed there for him! He quickly learned they weren't, as that was the same night The Beatles made their infamous United States premiere on television. Davy honestly and openly discussed the fact that many of the voices and instruments on The Monkees' hits were actually performed by other professional musicians. This fact actually led to the demise of The Monkees in that Peter Tork, Mickey Dolenz, and Michael Nesmith wanted to be taken seriously as musicians and began producing their own music and albums. That experiment didn't do too well, and The Monkees eventually broke up until their somewhat successful reunion tours some years later.

During the interview, I asked Davy, 'Did you make a lot of money as a Monkee?' Not surprisingly, he didn't. Most of the profits, as was the case often in those days, were eaten up by the record companies and the merchandising entities. Davy said that when they came off a tour, they would be billed for everything: meals, phone calls, and taxis, etc. In the end there wasn't much left over for them. Although, he says, he did make some money, it was nothing near what many thought he was earning.

Still, Davy remarked: 'You can't believe how great my life has been from being a member of The Monkees.'

Smokey Robinson – Singer/Songwriter, Member of the Rock 'N' Roll Hall of Fame

I couldn't believe that we had booked one of my favorite singer/songwriters of all time - the great Smokey Robinson! I was so excited to have him on the show. The interview was scheduled for what turned out to be a cold and rainy November day in NYC, and I was concerned that the nasty weather might affect Smokey's mood going into the interview. When he walked into the studio, he looked tired and uninterested in being there. One of my producers got him some tea and directed him to a comfortable sofa where he could unwind from the New York City traffic and pouring rain prior to the interview. Fifteen minutes later, he was directed to the set where I was - somehow, with all my excitement - sitting and waiting for him. At the time, Smokey was coming out with another one of his great albums, which his assistant handed to me. The assistant, who was nice but quite stern, must have reminded me at least ten times, 'Mickey, we're on a very tight schedule, so you have 25 minutes with Smokey – not a minute more.' I thought to myself, *I can live with that,* and felt fortunate to even have this wonderful opportunity of interviewing The Great Smokey Robinson.

Prior to the interview, I had read that Smokey was an avid golfer and that he was struggling with his putting, so the crew all chipped in and we purchased him a new Odyssey putter. Action - the cameras started to roll.

'Smokey Robinson, welcome to *Profiles*,' I began. 'Before we start the interview, the crew and I got together and want to give you this new Odyssey putter that will hopefully help you improve your putting.' Smokey was obviously touched and couldn't thank me and the crew enough for this thoughtful gift. Talk about an icebreaker - that was the Stanley Cup of ice breakers! From that point on, Smokey was all in and gave me a phenomenal interview throughout. It was sensitive, thought-provoking and interesting.

I had lost track of the time during the interview and at exactly the 25-minute mark, I could see Smokey's assistant out of the corner of my eye contorting herself almost cartoonishly and pointing at her watch. First, she would move to get my attention, then sprint around to the other side of the set to try Smokey. The woman was determined to stay on schedule, and neither myself nor Smokey were cooperating.

Suddenly, Smokey stopped the interview, turned to his assistant and growled, 'Sit down and be quiet, I'm talking with my brother Mickey. I'll let you know when we're finished.'

WOW! Well if that wasn't a green light for more interview time! In fact, the interview lasted almost an hour, and I couldn't stop grinning. We ended up having enough material to make a two-parter. I often wonder what role 'The Putter' played in the end result of this outstanding interview with Smokey...

Christopher Plummer - Actor and Oscar Winner

Two or three weeks prior to an interview, my assistant hands me a packet that includes the upcoming guest's press package, biography, recent newspaper and magazine articles, along with any other applicable material that will help me organize my interview. However, it was different with Mr. Plummer. As she handed me the usual research package, my assistant added: 'I've included a link to a recent radio interview that I think you should listen to.' At the time, Christopher was doing publicity for his autobiography titled *Christopher Plummer: In Spite of Myself* which spanned a hefty 656 pages. The host of the small radio station started, 'Christopher Plummer, welcome to WKRP in Cincinnati, Ohio. It's a pleasure having you on the show!' The interview started out okay as the host strolled Mr. Plummer through a series of what I would call 'warm-up' questions; then all of a sudden, Mr. Plummer asked the host 'Excuse me, son, did you read my book?' The host gave his best Jackie Gleason - humma, humma, humma - and said 'Not yet, but I'm planning to read it', to which Christopher responded... well, he didn't. All that was heard was the click of the phone line hanging up. He must have been offended - and understandably so!

At that moment, I realized that I'd better buckle down and start reading Mr. Plummer's autobiography, or suffer a similar fate. Now, when I said this book was hefty, I wasn't kidding. To say it was comparable to *The Rise and Fall of the Third Reich* would be no exaggeration, and there was no Audible back then. Though the book itself was enjoyable, I definitely had my work cut out for me.

The day of the interview had come, and I felt confident in my research.

'Christopher Plummer, welcome to *Profiles*,' I began. 'Mr. Plummer, would it be alright if I started the interview by reading a passage from your book?' Plummer's face broke out into a smile, 'God Bless you Mickey, absolutely!' Quickly he realized that I had read his book, and throughout the interview, he thanked me profusely for doing so. The key to getting into Carnegie Hall is 'practice, practice, practice', and I learned early on in my broadcasting career that the key to a great interview is 'research, research, research.' Nothing looks more uncomfortable than a host winging it without doing the necessary research. The Christopher Plummer interview was a great example of having to go the extra mile in the research department. The result was ample respect from Mr. Plummer and a phenomenal interview that remains priceless.

When I asked Christopher about his role in portraying Captain Von Trapp in the film *The Sound of Music*, he sarcastically snapped 'Von Trapp was a bore, next question.' I quickly changed the subject, 'So Christopher, how do you feel about awards in general?' 'I really don't think they're fair,' he replied. He went on to say, 'If I'm nominated for a dramatic role, I should be judged against others in dramatic roles, not comedy and drama - how can one do that?' Today, I wonder if his attitude might have softened a bit after having won the Academy Award for Best Supporting Actor at age 82 for his role in *Beginnings* in 2011. He remains both the oldest Academy Award Acting winner and nominee.

Tony Orlando - Singer and Entertainer

Former host of the *Tony Orlando and Dawn* TV series, Tony has
been a guest on *Profiles* twice, each time the interview lasting
over an hour. Without a doubt, Tony is one of the best
storytellers ever in show business. Ask him a question, and he
has a story associated with it. Additionally, he is one of the
nicest, most sincere celebrities I have ever had the pleasure of
meeting. Nothing is off limits, positive or negative - if it
happened in his life, he's willing to talk about it, without
reservation. He's a special guy, and besides being extremely
talented, his candidness has certainly been one of the keys to his
success. Tony was a teen idol at 16 years old with hits such as
'Halfway to Paradise' and 'Bless You'. He then met Clive Davis
and became a record executive in his early 20s. He later went on
to be one of the biggest TV stars of the 1970s with the *Tony
Orlando and Dawn Show* on CBS. Tony is half Greek and half
Puerto Rican and proudly calls himself a 'Greek-A-Rican'.
Dawn, comprised of Telma Hopkins and Joyce Vincent Wilson,
were both African Americans. They became the first multi-racial
group to have a prime-time television series. Of all of the
accomplishments Tony discussed during our second interview,
what he said he was most proud of was 'In three years of doing
the *Tony Orlando Show*, one year after Petula Clark kissed Harry
Belafonte on television to an uproar that echoed throughout the
nation, a Greek-A-Rican and two African American ladies never
received one - not one hate mail. That's the significance of what
we accomplished. The country was changing, and we were
changing with it.'

He also talked about having Jackie Gleason as his first guest
on the *Tony Orlando and Dawn Show*. During rehearsals, Tony
overheard Mr. Gleason make a racial remark about Telma and
Joyce and aggressively confronted him. Mr. Gleason walked off
the set, and it appeared that the premiere of *Tony Orlando and
Dawn* would have to go on without television's biggest star of
the time, Jackie Gleason. The fact that Tony would stand up to
the king of show business while still in his 20s speaks volumes

to the character of the man. Hours before the premiere of the series, Jackie Gleason walked into Tony's dressing room and apologized. The two would go on to be the closest of friends right up to Mr. Gleason's passing. In fact, before every episode, Mr. Gleason would call Tony and wish him good luck while critiquing his prior performances as a mentor. I have been equally as fortunate in considering Tony Orlando as my friend. You can call him with a problem, or even just to say hello, and within minutes he'll respond. As I've said: 'Tony Orlando is a special guy.'

Deepak Chopra - World Renowned Pioneer in Integrative Medicine and Personal Transformation

Time magazine has described Dr. Chopra as 'One of the Top 100 heroes & icons of the century.' Every so often, we've booked a guest on *Profiles* and I've immediately wondered to myself *Can I hold my own with this guest? Might I be over my head here?* Anticipating an interview with Deepak Chopra was definitely one of those times. Once again, research would have to play a major part in overcoming this self-doubt. After all, Dr. Chopra was one of, if not the, number one guest for Oprah Winfrey for years. Now it was my time. We talked about his 87 books, his transformation through meditation, and his legion of followers throughout the world. However, my goal was to get a side of the man seldom seen before. Ninety-nine percent of the interviews I'd seen focused more on his philosophies and works. I decided to talk about his family: his wife Rita, his daughter Malika and his son Gotham. I read quotes from his children and their feelings about his journey, at which Dr. Chopra lit up like a Christmas tree. I don't think anyone had ever discussed his children with him in depth. Malika is now an accomplished author, and Gotham an award-winning filmmaker for such projects as *Tom Vs. Time*, a documentary series focusing on the New England Patriots' quarterback Tom Brady.

Mr. Chopra had just released his latest book, titled *The Healing Self*, which chronicles a new plan to supercharge your immunity. I asked Mr. Chopra if our immune systems are facing a level of threat that is unprecedented. His response was, 'Principally, because of global travel, something that is happening in Bangladesh would be an epidemic in New York tomorrow.'

Dr. Chopra came to the United States from India in 1980 with just eight dollars in his pocket. Malika Chopra said, 'My parents are a wonderful example of living the American dream.' Dr. Chopra smiled and agreed, 'She's ABSOLUTELY right!'

Dr. Chopra began his residency in the U.S. at a hospital in Boston. 'I was stressed out, a smoker, and from time to time, I indulged in a drink or two,' he admitted. Then one day on his way home, he passed by a meditation center and decided to go in. For the first time in his life, he felt at total peace. 'It changed my life,' he recalled. Today, Dr. Chopra operates 'Chopra Centers' on both coasts, teaching meditation to the masses. He added, 'Six million people have been taught online by me and Oprah Winfrey in the last two years.'

With all that Dr. Chopra does career-wise, I asked him what he likes to do when he's not working. 'I'm an avid skier, a certified scuba diver, and I like to go into the wilderness each year for a week in silence.' I followed up by asking Dr. Chopra why someone should consider practicing meditation, and he calmly responded, 'It's a way to quiet the mind, and when the mind is quiet, the body gets quiet. When both work together, the healing response occurs.'

I then asked him what the best piece of advice he'd ever received was. He smiled and said 'From my mother: "Know what your unique gifts are, and then use them to serve the world. The best way to get rid of an enemy is to increase their capacity for wellbeing and happiness. Then they'll be your friend." '

'Motivation is mental, and inspiration is spiritual, and once you're inspired there's no going back.' Dr. Chopra left me with this wisdom and a refreshed sense of inspiration. The time I spent with him was truly enlightening!

Robert Wagner – Film and Television Actor

I was so excited to learn that we had booked Robert Wagner for *Profiles*. I, like many other baby boomers, spent the 60s, 70s, and 80s watching Mr. Wagner star on various television series such as *It Takes a Thief, Switch* and *Hart to Hart*. He was the prototype of what a Hollywood star should be: good looking, charming, charismatic, versatile, and always with that twinkle in his eyes that had the ladies swooning. He was the total package. As he sat in the chair opposite of me, I was fully aware that I was seated just across from Hollywood greatness. Here was an actor whose mentors were Clark Gable and Spencer Tracy. He was a movie star first in films such as *The Pink Panther, A Kiss Before Dying* and *The Longest Day* before he moved over to television. During our interview, he expressed his reluctance to venture into television; after all, as he said: 'I was a movie star.' Robert felt that a move into television could be a jump-the-shark moment in an already illustrious career. Nevertheless, he took the leap in 1968, and over the next three decades, became one of the biggest stars in television history.

We also discussed his marriage to the beautiful actress Natalie Wood, who drowned off Caramel Bay in 1981. The two first married in 1957, when Wood was just nineteen and Wagner nine years her senior. Despite enjoying a reputation as one of Hollywood's most celebrated couples, their relationship had its ups and downs, including Wood's reportedly contentious relationship with heartthrob actor Warren Beatty.

During our interview, I read a quote from Wagner's 2009 book release *Pieces of My Heart: A Life* where he wrote that he was so irate with Beatty that he waited outside his house for three days with a gun. I then asked Wagner if his intent was to kill Beatty, and he replied with honesty, 'Yes, I was pretty upset at the time.' Thank goodness Beatty never showed up. Wagner and Wood divorced in 1962, only to remarry again a decade later. During their time apart, Wagner said, 'Natalie was never really out of my heart.' We finished the interview talking about Wagner's recent roles as the eye-patch-wearing henchman

'Number Two' in the *Austin Powers* trilogy of films, opposite Mike Myers. Wagner reminisced that the role gave new life to his acting career while gaining an enormous new following. Wagner chuckled, 'I've been in the movie business for sixty years, and now I'm known as Number Two.'

I found Robert Wagner to be an old school gentleman, polished to the core. It was an honor to spend time with him on the show.

Darlene Love – Singer and Actress

We've had Darlene on *Profiles* a total of three times. I had been a big fan since she first gained prominence in the early 60s with her mega-hit 'He's A Rebel', and I've always loved her vocals on the celebrated 1963 Christmas album *A Christmas Gift for You from Phil Spector*.

I found Darlene to be one of the sweetest, most genuine celebrities I had interviewed on *Profiles*. No subject was out of bounds, including Phil Spector, who is currently in jail on a murder conviction. Darlene had two problems with Phil: for starters, he never paid her properly for her vocals on many of Spector's produced hits, including his popular Christmas album that generated millions. Eventually, Darlene did receive proper restitution, but only after a long and arduous court trial. Secondly, Darlene always felt that it was Phil, who was on the voting board of the Rock 'N' Roll Hall of Fame Committee, that kept her from induction for a long period of time. He was upset that Darlene had the gall to take him to court over the recordings royalties she deserved and was being denied. After Phil was sentenced to jail on his murder conviction, Darlene was immediately inducted into the 2011 Class of Honorees to The Rock 'N' Roll of Fame. What a coincidence!

In the early 70s, Darlene moved to L.A. and took a break from her singing in order to raise a family after singing jobs had dried up a bit for her. In order to make ends meet, she took work as a maid in Beverly Hills. As Darlene described: 'I had to park my Mercedes that I had bought from my singing days around the block so as not to let my clients think I was living a high maintenance lifestyle.'

Then one day, while she was cleaning toilets in one of these homes, she heard her classic song 'Christmas (Baby Please Come Home)' come on the radio. 'Right there I took this as a sign from God that I needed to change my life and go back to singing,' Darlene said.

Love returned to music in the early 80s and to an adoring audience that she thought had long forgotten her. Steven Van Zandt had caught one of her performances at The Roxy in L.A. and convinced her to return to New York City and continue with her career there.

She took his advice and hasn't stopped working since. Her recent work in acting includes playing Danny Glover's wife Trish Murtaugh in all four *Lethal Weapon* movies, and on Broadway she holds many starring roles in various productions including such musicals as *Grease* and *Hairspray*.

However, singing is what Darlene always did best! From 1986 through 2014, she would appear on the last episode before Christmas on *Late Night with David Letterman* to perform her song 'Christmas (Baby Please Come Home)'. Paul Schafer and the band made the production bigger and bigger with each passing year, and Darlene, whose voice only seemed to improve with age, never disappointed. As I told Darlene many times, 'It just isn't Christmas without hearing you perform that song.'

Joe Montana – NFL Quarterback

What a thrill, learning that we had booked four-time Super Bowl Champion and three-time Super Bowl MVP, quarterback Joe Montana, for *Profiles*.

The interview was to be conducted at a hotel in New Jersey where Joe would be participating in a Sports Memorabilia event the following day. The interview was scheduled for 5pm. We were instructed by Joe's people to arrive for set-up at 3:30pm.

When we arrived, we were led to Joe's suite and were told that Joe was in transit and would be arriving at 5pm for the interview, which gave us ample time for our set-up of the lights, sound, and cameras, etc. During the set-up, I noticed a nice spread of cold cuts, salads, and breads in a corner of the room. I thought to myself, *How nice of them to provide this for myself and my crew.* After the set-up was complete, we helped ourselves to the food, then sat back and awaited Joe's arrival. At approximately 4:45, Joe's assistant walked in and introduced himself to our crew. After a glance around the suite, he asked, 'Who ate Joe's dinner?' Talk about feeling like a kid who got his hand caught in the cookie jar - my face paled as a common proverb came to mind - assuming something only makes an ass of u and me!

Joe walked in at 5pm, and the first thing out of my mouth was a slew of apologies. Joe laughed, 'Don't worry about it, I would never eat that food. We're going out to an Italian restaurant after the interview.' I could have drowned in that wave of relief.

My first impression of Joe Montana was that physically he was much smaller than expected in height and stature for one of the greats in NFL history, but what he lacked in stature, he certainly made up for in character. It was his ability to remain calm under pressure that helped his teams to 32 fourth quarter come-from-behind victories. He was appropriately nicknamed 'Joe Cool' and 'The Comeback Kid.'

We discussed his game-winning touchdown pass in the 1981 NFL Championship Game against the Dallas Cowboys, so memorable that it would become known simply as 'The Catch'. Of which, Joe said, 'I know it's hard to believe but we practiced that play all the time.'

Many of his passes were caught by wide receiver Jerry Rice, who is widely considered to be the greatest wide receiver in NFL history. According to Montana, 'What made Jerry so great was that every day in practice, everything he did was at full speed. He practiced at the same speed and intensity he exhibited during the games.' It was a thrill sitting down with the great Joe Montana, and he exhibited the same poise during the interview that he exhibited in the NFL for 16 seasons. Joe was elected to the Pro Football Hall of Fame in 2000, in his first year of eligibility.

Judy Collins – Singer/Songwriter

I adored my interview with musical icon Judy Collins. I can't remember any other guest being as outspoken, heartfelt, and compelling as Judy was on a number of sensitive topics such as alcoholism and suicide.

As a singer, Judy has experienced international prominence since the 1960s with hits such as 'Both Sides Now', written for her by Joni Mitchell. The song also won Collins her first Grammy Award. Other hits would follow: 'Someday Soon' 'Chelsea Morning' and 'Amazing Grace'. However, her biggest success came in 1975, when she recorded Stephen Sondheim's 'Send in The Clowns', from her best-selling album *Judith*. The single spent 27 weeks on the *Billboard* pop singles chart, earning Collins a Grammy Award Nomination for best pop vocal performance, while earning Sondheim a Grammy for Song of the Year.

Although Collins had experienced such success and fame through her music, she also had a dark side. For years, she battled an addiction to alcohol, and she is more than willing to talk about it. She opened up about the damage it did to her personally, as well as to her musical life, and how the addiction contributed to her struggle with depression. Judy admitted during our interview that she had tried other drugs back in the 1960s, but alcohol had always been her main vice.

I asked Judy about what she referred to as The Irish Virus, referring to her bouts with alcohol. She explained, 'For a long time it was just part of the scenery, I knew I was an alcoholic since I was 19. So if I was going to be an alcoholic, I was going to do it right.'

I then asked Judy, regarding her battle with alcohol abuse, 'At the worst of it, how bad was it?' Judy responded, '37 years ago, I was really cooked, terribly sick. I had alcohol destroy my life.' She went on to say, 'I went into treatment 37 years ago and got lucky, I was fortunate that the compulsion to drink was lifted right out of me.'

Today, Judy does all the things that help her stay sober; however, according to Judy, 'I'm thrilled to be sober, but it is a whole different life.' From there we jumped into the subject of suicide. Her son, Clark, succumbed to suicide at the age of 33 in 1997. She had written about the experience in her best-selling book, *Sanity and Grace*, which she wrote to help others going through a similar tragedy. Judy said, 'I had to write about it to get through it to find some light after the darkness.'

We discussed the fact that annually 40,000 people a year commit suicide in the United States, 8,000 of which are associated with the military. 'Suicide is a mental health issue. However, there are ways to deal with it. Know the trigger points of loved ones who may have suicidal tendencies, so you can get them into treatment before it's too late,' Collins states.

Today, Judy continues to record and perform all over the world. She does about a hundred dates a year. She has maintained her sobriety since the late 1970s.

Chapter 8
Profiles Lasting Impressions

Every *Profiles* episode always seems to leave a lasting impression; be it something that happened before, during, or after the interview, there is always a part of each that is firmly etched in my memory forever. Sometimes, it's the smallest thing that remains with you. In this chapter, I'll be sharing with you a few of those lasting impressions.

Dion Di Mucci – Singer, Songwriter

Known mononymously as Dion, I had grown up listening to his hits such as 'The Wanderer', 'Ruby Baby' and 'Runaround Sue', and on his 60th birthday, we had scheduled an interview with him at The Hard Rock Café near Times Square in NYC. Dion was inducted into the Rock 'N' Roll Hall of Fame in 1989. He was a musical icon, and I was about to interview him, on his 60th birthday no less. As we greeted each other, I was pleased to see that he was full of personality and as sharp as ever. As he sat down across from me holding his guitar, I thought to myself, *Maybe we'll get lucky and he'll play a little for us* - and lucky we were! Throughout the interview, he played us bits and pieces of songs from a new album he was about to release. It was an incredible unplugged interview.

When I asked Dion about being part of the ill-fated 'Winter Dance Party' tour with Buddy Holly, Ritchie Valens, and the Big Bopper, to say his mood became pensive would be an understatement. With a tear in his eye, he was willing to talk about the day the music died. According to Dion: 'We were touring the Midwest in the dead of winter on an old school bus with a broken heater; I had never experienced cold like that before.' After a concert stop in Clear Lake, Iowa, Holly and Valens began getting sick so Holly and the others decided to charter a flight to the next venue rather than travel on the freezing cold tour bus. Buddy Holly invited Dion to accompany the group on the plane, but Dion decided to pass. 'When Buddy invited me to join him, I asked him, how much? Buddy replied, Thirty-six dollars each.' Dion leaned back, sighing deeply. 'Ya know, if it were thirty-five or even forty, I probably wouldn't have given it a second thought. But thirty-six dollars was the exact amount my mother was paying for her rent in the Bronx, and I just couldn't justify the indulgence.' Instead, Dion headed back to the bus, and on February 3rd, 1959, Buddy Holly, Ritchie Valens, and the Big Bopper (J.P. Richardson) headed for the airport to join pilot Roger Peterson. The plane crashed shortly into the flight, killing all on board. Today, in his late 70s, Dion continues to record and perform throughout the country.

Gloria Gaynor – Singer

We had Gloria Gaynor on *Profiles* twice, and each interview with her was a pleasure. She is lovely, and incredibly down to earth. In a way, Gloria had two careers. The first was in the mid-70s when she was signed to Columbia Records by Clive Davis. Her first album *Never Can Say Goodbye* featured three songs on the first side ('Honey Bee' 'Never Can Say Goodbye' and 'Reach Out, I'll Be There') with no break between the songs. This 19-minute dance marathon proved to be enormously popular, especially at dance clubs such as Studio 54. Her second career blossomed with the emergence of the disco era with her 1979 mega-hit 'I Will Survive'.

Interestingly, 'I Will Survive' was originally released as the B-side of 'Substitute'. A Boston DJ decided to turn the record over and 'I Will Survive' played through the radio speakers of anyone tuned in. The massive audience response was so positive, it forced the record company to flip the songs, so that subsequent copies of the single listed the more popular song on the A-side. 'I Will Survive' was not only a number one hit but also became the anthem of the disco movement nationwide.

As we discussed 'I Will Survive', I reminded Gloria that the song had become something of an ode to female emancipation. Many feel the lyrics of the song were written from the point of view of a woman, recently dumped, telling her former lover that she can cope without him and wants nothing more to do with him - go on, now go!

That wasn't how Gloria saw it. During a performance at the Beacon Theater some weeks before recording 'I Will Survive' she had slipped onstage over a monitor and broke her back. She admits that even during the recording itself, she was still in a great deal of pain and had trouble moving freely. There was a period where she thought she might never be able to walk again. However, through an operation and diligent rehabilitation, she eventually fully recovered. Gloria stated: 'For me, the meaning of 'I Will Survive' was reflecting on coming back and overcoming my broken back.'

In 1980, 'I Will Survive' received the Grammy Award for best disco recording, the only year that award was given. The category was eliminated the following year, due in part to the anti-disco movement through the country.

La Toya Jackson – Singer, Author

I really liked LaToya. Reflecting back, I'm not even sure what my expectations were prior to meeting her. I just remembered upon saying goodbye, I liked her. I found her to be sweet, sincere, and candid.

The fifth child of the Jackson family, Latoya had carved out an impressive show business career as a singer, songwriter, actress, author, businesswoman, and television personality.

Going into the interview, I knew her life hadn't been easy - just trying to follow in the footsteps of Michael and Janet would be enough for most to spend a life in therapy. Additionally, in the 1990s, she had to survive an abusive marriage at the hands of her manager, Jack Gordon. Thankfully, that marriage finally ended in divorce in 1997.

Latoya was on a promotional tour with her second memoir, titled *Starting Over*, in the spring of 2011. In the book, she pays tribute to her late brother, Michael Jackson, who had passed a couple of years earlier. She also shed light on her own journey of domestic abuse, hoping that the new book release might help others suffering the same fate.

'People who are being abused, whether it be physical or mental, must do something about it immediately. Many don't know where to turn. When it happens once, it's going to happen again. There are people and places out there that victims can go to for help,' Jackson said.

Latoya's abuse at the hands of her husband, which was both mental and physical, lasted for several years. 'For the longest time, I didn't understand that abuse is a universal horror that happens to women of every race, religion, and social class. I was so ashamed that I let it happen to me, so I tried to pretend that it didn't.'

'Why did you stay in an abusive marriage for so long?' I asked her.

She quickly responded: 'They instill such a fear in you. He had so much control and power over me I felt I couldn't leave.'

During the interview we also discussed her brother Michael's death, and that he had expressed to her his fear that he was going to be killed, weeks and months prior to his death.

'Michael happened to own one of the largest music publishing catalogs in the world. He owned all the Beatles material and just about every artist you can think of. Every time one of those songs got played, he got paid for it. He was raking in millions, year after year. There were others who wanted to control it and wanted to get him out of the way, and he knew it. That's what he was afraid of,' Latoya said. 'When I finally realized that Michael was dead, my immediate thought was not "how did Michael die?" but "who killed Michael?"'

'Who stood the most to gain from his death?' I asked Latoya.

'Everybody who wanted that music library. Everybody that he surrounded himself with. The people who came into his circle less than a week before his passing. They're the ones who stood the most to gain. If you follow the money trail, you know what happened to my brother,' Latoya responded.

'How would you like your brother Michael to be remembered?'

'What a lot of people don't know is that Michael is in the *Guinness Book of World Records* for donating to the most charities ever in the world. He's given over four hundred million dollars of his own personal money to different charities, and he didn't want to take credit for it.' Latoya beamed with pride. Towards the end of the interview, I asked Latoya, 'Do you feel the complete truth regarding Michael's death will ever be revealed as you see it?'

'I'm going to do my best to continue to investigate until the truth is revealed,' Latoya snapped.

In March of 1989, Latoya posed for a pictorial and appeared on the cover of *Playboy* magazine, which evolved into a huge bestseller for *Playboy*.

Reflecting back, Latoya remembered: 'I was extremely embarrassed by the photos. I was pressured and misled by my husband to do it. All the people at *Playboy* thought I was the ridiculous thing, I thought that I'd be posing in a nightgown. It took days for me to take anything off. It was a work of art to get me to do this.'

Eric Roberts – Actor

One of Hollywood's edgier, more intriguing characters for decades. After a bushel of breakout roles in the late 1970s and 80s, Eric appeared to be on the threshold of becoming a bankable Hollywood leading man. He had remarkable talent, and could, with the ease of a chameleon, shift into a variety of roles - good guy, bad guy, regular grey area guy - all with convincing success. Unfortunately, the actor fell to substance abuse, leading to a near-fatal car accident that put him in a coma for three days, left some facial scars, and caused some neurological damage that he overcame after months of therapy.

It wasn't just physical damage that came of his dangerous vices; the drugs made him a nasty person, and his relationships, both professional and personal, suffered for it.

'When you treat people as badly as I did, they will all rise up from the ashes eventually and get even,' Roberts said during our interview. He also discussed his being estranged from his sister, mega-star Julia Roberts. He said he understood why she felt the way she did, but hoped that one day he could make things right with her and her family once again.

By the end of the interview, I couldn't help but root for the guy. Despite the many mistakes he's made in his life and career, he's owned up to them, accepting the consequences without complaints, bitterness or excuses. He's just elated that at this stage of his life, enough people are willing to forgive his past and allow him to continue to pursue his passion for acting.

Roberts' leading man aspirations may not have taken full flight, but the man still makes waves in the industry. In fact, the day of our interview, he was excited to learn that he had won a role in Christopher Nolan's *The Dark Knight*. As of this writing, he's credited with four hundred eighty-seven film and television appearances. Undoubtedly, he is among the most prolific American actors with the most film credits of all time.

Tommy James – Singer/Songwriter

We've had Tommy James on *Profiles* three times spanning over 15 years. Tommy was one of the most successful singer/songwriters of the late 60s. According to Tommy, 'Our goal was to produce one hit after another', and like few others, he succeeded! His first, 'Hanky Panky', started out as a regional hit in Pittsburg and eventually became a national top ten single. Having garnered the attention of many of the top labels residing in New York City, Tommy headed for the Big Apple to make his best record deal. But as soon as he touched ground in NYC, he got a call - one label after the other decided not to sign Tommy. He later learned that Morris Levy, President of Roulette Records and a person with close ties to the Genovese Crime Family, took a liking to Tommy and told all the other labels, one by one, "He's mine!"; and so it was that Tommy James and his Shondells became a major player in the music business under the Roulette label. Many hits would follow 'Hanky Panky', such as 'I Think We're Alone Now', 'Crimson and Clover', 'Mirage' and 'Mony Mony'. Of Morris Levy's leadership, James said: 'He knew a hit when he heard it, and that's not as easy as it sounds.'

Reflecting back on Morris' business dealings, Tommy said: 'Morris had about three sets of books and was constantly being audited by the IRS. I was on a first name basis with many of the agents because they lived at the Roulette offices in New York City.' When Morris originally signed Tommy he told him 'Buckle up kid, you're about to go on one hell of a ride!'

I asked Tommy, 'Was he right?' He replied, 'Absolutely!'

In 2010, Tommy released his memoir *Me, The Mob and The Music*. It was an instant best seller. The book is now in production for a major film release.

I had to ask Tommy about one of my favorite songs of his, 'Mony Mony'. 'How did you come up with the name?' Tommy laughed and said, 'We were finished with the music for the song but couldn't come up with a name, when all of a sudden I glanced at the New York City skyline from my apartment and noticed in all its glory, a brightly lit sign that read 'Mutual of New York'. I then turned to my group and said: 'Mony, Mony!' It was like a voice from God.'

In 1982 British rocker Billy Idol released a cover of 'Mony, Mony'. It was a huge hit for Billy, just as it was for Tommy years before. Besides Billy Idol, tons of artists have covered Tommy James' songs - over three hundred to be exact. Among them include Bruce Springsteen, Joan Jett, Dolly Parton, and Tom Jones, to mention a few.

Tommy has yet to be inducted into the Rock 'N' Roll Hall of Fame. I know this bothers him, and certainly, he's more than deserving of the honor, but Tommy has too much class to speak negatively of the organization and its political board of directors. One can only hope that he gets his due and will be inducted in the not too distant future. He belongs among the greats because his body of work more than illustrates his greatness.

Tony Iommi – Guitar God

Tony was on his book tour in 2012 for the release of his autobiography *Iron Man: My Journey Through Heaven and Hell with Black Sabbath* when we were contacted by his book publisher to schedule him for a guest appearance on *Profiles*. Going in, I knew very little about Tony, or, for that matter, Black Sabbath. I had never been a fan of heavy metal music. All I knew was that Tony was the guitar player behind frontman Ozzy Osbourne. During my research and after speaking with several metal fans, I realized that in those circles, Tony Iommi is considered not only a guitar god but also as one of the legends of heavy metal.

'How did you meet Ozzy?' I asked.

Tony giggled, 'I was looking for a singer for my new band when I noticed a flyer in the local record store - Singer looking for gig.'

With another band member in tow, Tony quickly took down the information and went to investigate the advertised wannabe singer. Upon their arrival, they were greeted by Osbourne himself. Immediately, Tony knew this would never work. 'I had known Ozzy from high school, and I whispered to my bandmate, 'I'm pretty sure he can't sing'. Boy, was I wrong!' Tony's only criticism of Ozzy was 'Early on during touring, Ozzy was a bit stiff on stage; once he loosened up, he was awesome.'

'How did you come up with the name Black Sabbath?' I asked Tony.

'When we started out, we were called Earth. We showed up for a gig somewhere outside of London, and when we arrived, there was another band on stage with the same name; they had double booked. Right then, we knew we had to change our name. Some weeks later, we spotted a poster for the film *Black Sabbath* starring Boris Karloff and it clicked!'

During the interview, I noticed one of Tony's fingers on his left hand was missing a tip below the nail. He explained that just before he decided to make music and tour a full-time gig, he first had to give up his daytime job working in a local factory cutting sheet metal. On his last day, he came home from work for lunch and didn't want to return. However, his mother forced him to return to the factory to finish his workday. Distracted, he accidentally sliced off the tip to one of his fingers in the machinery.

In the years following the accident, Tony had to get creative with the way he played. Turns out those leather fingertips aren't just a fashion statement.

He also developed a unique sound that made Black Sabbath one of the most successful heavy metal bands of all time.

Leslie Caron – Actress

It was in the winter of 2010 when I was informed that we had booked legendary actress and dancer Leslie Caron for *Profiles*. Leslie was on a book tour promoting the release of her autobiography, titled *Thank Heaven*. I was extremely excited to have her on the show, especially since *Gigi* was one of my favorite musicals of all time. During the interview, I asked Leslie about her thoughts on *Gigi*, to which she responded: 'Of any musical ever made, I think that film was the closest to perfection.' I couldn't agree more!

Leslie was a dancer way before she became an actress. She is one of the few dancers/actresses to have danced with Gene Kelly, Fred Astaire, Mikhail Baryshnikov, and Rudolf Nureyev.

Born and raised in France, Leslie was discovered by Gene Kelly while performing as a ballerina in Paris. Impressed with her beauty and talents, he immediately cast her to appear opposite him in the musical *An American in Paris* (1951). Reflecting back, Caron said: 'At the time I didn't even know who Gene Kelly was.' This role led to a long-term MGM contract and a sequence of films which included *The Glass Slipper* and the drama *The Man with a Cloak*.

At the time of our interview, Leslie was in her late 70s, and I found the years had only refined her sense of grace and charm. I was curious and asked her if her mother had given her any advice when leaving France for the bright lights of Hollywood, to which she responded: 'My mother told me whatever you do in America, don't marry Mickey Rooney!'

Although she took her mother's advice and steered clear of the renowned vaudevillian, Leslie did have a much-publicized relationship with Hollywood heartthrob Warren Beatty. I'd read somewhere that Warren had proposed to Leslie, and that he very much wanted to marry her. When I asked Leslie about it, she said: 'He was too controlling, with too much drama. So I decided not to marry Warren.'

In 1953, Leslie was nominated for an Academy Award for Best Actress for her starring role in the film *Gigi*, and in 2007, earned a Primetime Emmy Award for her guest performance on *Law and Order: Special Victims Unit*. When I asked Leslie about her incredible body of work, she laughed: 'It's just work, we all have to work at something.'

For her extensive contributions to the film industry, Leslie was inducted into the Hollywood Walk of Fame on December 8th 2009 with a motion picture star located at 6153 Hollywood Boulevard.

Duane 'Dog' Chapman – Bounty Hunter

In the fall of 2007, the famous Bounty Hunter Duane 'Dog' Chapman was scheduled for an interview on *Profiles*. At the time, he was at the height of his success with his reality television series *Dog the Bounty Hunter*, which aired on A&E.

No one was more elated with his celebrity status than 'The Dog', especially with his criminal background. In 1967, Duane was convicted of first-degree murder and sentenced to five years in a Texas prison. He explained during our interview: 'I was waiting in a car when my friend accidentally killed a drug dealer in a struggle to buy some cannabis.' He went on to explain, 'Back then, if someone you're with steals a candy bar, you're just as guilty. It was the law in Texas. So I went to prison for that.'

In my research, I had read mention that Chapman has recurring nightmares, so I asked him what he thought triggered these nightmares. He replied: 'I wonder still today if maybe this is all a dream and I am sitting in the electric chair, and as I'm breathing my last few breaths, I think: life is so good, is this really happening to me or is it all a dream?' While serving his 18 months at Texas State Penitentiary in Huntsville, Texas, Chapman served as the Warden's barber. One day while serving his sentence, he tackled an inmate about to be shot trying to escape. Correction officers complimented him for his actions. It was their remarks that inspired him to become a bounty hunter upon his parole in January of 1979. Interestingly, because of his felony conviction, Chapman is not allowed to own a firearm. Instead, he has always used a taser or Mace to apprehend criminals when necessary.

'How important do you feel bounty hunting is to the success of the criminal justice system?' I asked. Without hesitation, he answered: 'If you had more cops you wouldn't need bounty hunters. The cops are busy getting the kids home safe, they're busy, the bank just got robbed, they got to go, they can't be looking for John Doe. If there were more cops there wouldn't need to be bounty hunters.'

In 2007, Chapman released his autobiography, titled *You Can Run, But You Can't Hide*. The book debuted at number one on the *New York Times* bestseller list.

Kenny G – Musician/Saxophonist

In the spring of 2015, Kenny G was in New York City promoting his latest album, *Brazilian Nights*. According to Kenny, the album was inspired by bossa nova recordings of Cannonball Adderley, Stan Getz, and Paul Desmond. The album once again had Kenny back on the *Billboard* charts.

As I prepared for the interview I was well aware that Kenny G was the biggest-selling instrumental musician of the modern era and one of the best-selling artists of all time, with global sales totaling more than seventy-five million records. When he walked onto the set, the first thing I noticed was his distinctive long hair, a trademark that hasn't changed since his emergence onto the music scene in the late 1970s. Immediately, I found Kenny to be pleasant, friendly and accommodating.

Kenny began his professional career in 1973 at 17 years old and still in high school as a sideman for Barry White's Love Unlimited Orchestra. I asked Kenny what it was like working with the legendary Barry White. With a grin, he responded, 'I never met him. I just showed up at the recording sessions, played my part and I was out of there. But I loved Barry White.' That question sparked another memory of his days in Las Vegas playing in the orchestra behind Liberace.

'It was amazing. Every night Liberace came out, played the same songs and told the same stories word for word. I never met him as well, I was just one of the guys in the band,' Kenny recalled.

The one thing Kenny and I had in common was our love for golf, as we are both avid golfers. I had caught Kenny once or twice on television playing in the celebrity pro-am tournaments and was always impressed with his talent around the links. In fact, he's listed as a scratch golfer among celebrities who play golf. This basically means that on any given day he's capable of shooting even par, a tremendous accomplishment for any golfer. I asked Kenny how he could be so good at golf with such little time to practice with his hectic touring schedule. 'It's about the quality of my practice, when I do find the time,' Kenny explained. 'When I practice, I focus totally on my short game. Chipping and putting; that's where you save the most strokes.'

I had read somewhere that Kenny once played a round of golf with Tiger Woods and Phil Mickelson, two of the greatest players in the game. So I had to ask Kenny if he had learned anything playing alongside these two giants. Without hesitation, Kenny answered: 'The way they recover from bad shots - they're amazing! After errant shots, they come right back with great shots. Something every amateur can learn from. Keep your focus and never give up on a hole.'

In 1997, Kenny G earned a place in the *Guinness Book for World Records* for playing the longest note ever recorded on a saxophone. Using circular breathing, Kenny held an E-Flat for 45 minutes and 47 seconds at J.R Music World in New York City. When I asked Kenny about it, he laughed and said: 'That was such a stupid record, but it was pretty cool being in that book.'

During our interview, Kenny graced us with a demonstration of his legendary saxophone. 'This is the saxophone I got in high school. Back then it cost me three hundred dollars. Today, the same saxophone is going for about three thousand dollars.'

He went on to say: 'They've made newer models, but this is the one I prefer. I've used it on almost every recording I've ever made.'

Today, Kenny G continues to play his trusty old saxophone to sold-out audiences around the world.

Susan Lucci - Actress

Susan Lucci became famous for portraying Erica Kane on the ABC daytime drama *All My Children* for forty years, from 1970 to 2011. During that span, she has more than maintained her beauty and fitness. *TV Guide* recently placed Susan among its Fifty Greatest TV Stars Of All-Time.

The day of our interview was a hot and humid July day in New York City, and the air conditioning in our studio was below par that day. I remember Susan's hair beginning to lose its perfection during the interview, and I'm sure she realized it as well. I'll never forget her professionalism; not once did she complain or bring attention to the situation. Instead, she kept her focus and remained professional throughout our 50-minute interview. Many other celebrities of her stature might have complained and whined at the lack of proper air conditioning that day - but not Susan. What she did do was demonstrate the resilience and class that made her a survivor and legend.

For a good portion of her career, Susan had become notoriously synonymous with never winning an Emmy. We discussed the night she hosted NBC's *Saturday Night Live*, a show that had won tons of Emmys. Susan recalled: 'During my monologue, the show's cast and crew nonchalantly carried their Emmys on stage, using them as hammers and door jams, it was really funny.'

Totaling at twenty, Susan has more Emmy nominations than any other performer in the history of television, daytime or primetime. In May of 1999, Susan finally won an Emmy Award for Best Actress that had eluded her through nineteen previous nominations. 'When I finally won my Emmy, I really wasn't prepared. I got so used to losing that in 1999, I had nothing prepared to say, had I won.' Lucci went on to say, 'When they called my name, my main concern was not to leave anyone out, and to thank all those I needed to acknowledge.' It was a historic moment, not only for Lucci, but for all of television.

Our Susan Lucci interview also marked our 400th episode milestone. It was a special occasion for us and having Susan Lucci as our 400th episode guest made it all the more special. The last question I ask every guest who appears on *Profiles* is 'What do you hope that your legacy will be?' Susan beamed and proudly proclaimed: 'I think I will always be remembered for Erica Kane.'

Engelbert Humperdinck - Singer

What a thrill it was having singer Engelbert Humperdinck as a guest on *Profiles*. I had been a big fan of his music since the late 60s. His hits, such as 'Release Me', 'The Last Waltz', and 'After the Lovin', have all certainly stood the test of time.

Our interview with Engelbert took place in the spring of 2015. When he walked into our studio, my initial impression was that he was charming, with a great sense of humor. The first thing we discussed was his name, Engelbert Humperdinck. How did he get it? Enge, as friends call him, explained: 'I began my career as Jerry Dorsey for almost a decade, in the mid 60s. My manager, Gordon Mills, suggested a name-change to Engelbert Humperdinck, borrowed from the German 19th century composer of operas. The name worked.'

Interestingly, Gordon Mills was also the manager of singer Tom Jones. Both Engelbert and Tom were extremely successful by the late 60s. There was also an intense rivalry between them. Ironically, he ended up leaving his manager Gordon Mills because he felt Gordon was giving Tom Jones more attention. Reflecting back Engelbert said: 'I regret that. In addition, getting out of our contract cost me a lot of money.'

Over his illustrious career, Humperdinck has sold more than 150 million records worldwide. His good looks and easygoing style have garnered him a huge following, especially among women. Along the way, many have referred to him as a crooner, which never sat well with him. 'No crooner has the range I have. I can hit notes a bank could not cash. What I'd like to be described as is a contemporary singer, and a stylish performer.' During our interview, Engelbert said that he learned a great deal from watching Elvis on stage. 'He never took himself that serious,' Engelbert explained. One of his favorite Hollywood friends was Dean Martin. 'He was the greatest. I had lunch with Dean almost every week up until his death,' Engel said. 'He would never call me by my name. It was either Humpty Dumpty, or Dumpty Bumpy - anything but Engelbert. I loved him.'

In 2004, Engelbert released his autobiography, titled *Engelbert: What's In A Name?* The book was a best seller and unusually honest. In the book, Engel mentioned that he might have made love to over 2000 women. When I asked him if that was accurate, he responded: 'I think Jay Leno summed it up best when he said, "less work for your wife." ' We also discussed the Holmby Hills home he purchased in 1976, once owned by the late movie star Jane Mansfield, who was killed in a car accident in 1967. 'I purchased the house without ever stepping inside. I decided to buy it after looking at a few photos,' he said. Engelbert has since moved on. However, before he did, he had the house repainted bright pink, the way it was when Jane Mansfield lived there.

Verne Lundquist - Sportscaster

It was an honor having the opportunity to sit down with legendary sportscaster Verne Lundquist, who has spent the last 50 years calling some of the greatest moments in sports. As one of the most recognizable voices and faces in sports, Lundquist has covered more than twenty different sports during his illustrious career. Though I remembered Verne best for his work calling college football and basketball games, as the avid golfer that I am, I was more than familiar with his work on CBS, calling a historic 32 Masters golf tournaments.

During the interview, Verne mentioned that his two favorite Masters highlights were Tiger Woods' astounding comeback at the 2005 Masters, and Jack Nicklaus' legendary one-stroke victory at the 1986 Masters. In 2005, Verne was calling a play at the 16th hole where Tiger made his famous one hundred foot chip in from off the green. According to Lundquist, 'It was the most remarkable shot in golf that I have ever witnessed. After the ball went in I simply shouted 'OH WOW!' followed by, 'In your life have you ever seen anything like that.' That clip and Verne's call continues to be replayed thousands of times across the world each year.

In 1986, Verne was calling play at the 17th hole when Jack Nicklaus was making a legendary comeback on the back nine. 'I've never seen a crowd interacting with an athlete the way they did with Jack that day,' Verne exclaimed. 'I've never heard a noise level from the crowd that I witnessed in 1986, everyone was behind Jack.'

Nicklaus was tied for the lead and hit a great approach shot 18 feet below the hole. As Jack stood over his 18-footer for birdie, Verne remembered a piece of advice he had received from CBS Golf Producer Frank Chickanian: 'Let the picture tell the story.' For the 14 seconds it took Jack to hit the putt and for the ball to roll in the hole, 'I said nothing,' Lundquist recalls. 'I shouted "Yes sir!" and then remained silent for another 27 seconds, letting the picture tell the story.' It was one of the most iconic moments in golf, and, for that matter, in sports, and Lundquist was right in the middle of it.

Known as 'The Golden Throat', along with his trademark humility, Lundquist's goal was to always make the athlete the legend instead of the call itself. When I asked Verne what the key to his success as a sportscaster has been he answered, 'I have always seen myself as a teller of stories and not the story itself.' I'm convinced that it was this philosophy that earned Lundquist a Lifetime Achievement Award at the 37th Annual Sports Emmy awards.

In 1996, Lundquist was offered a part in the now-famous golf-themed film *Happy Gilmore* starring Adam Sandler. Verne's role was that of the announcer. 'When I arrived on the set I was handed my script. I immediately noticed that someone had crossed out Pat Summerall's name and penciled in mine. I guess Pat was their first choice and declined. Thank you, Mr. Summerall, that film is the gift that keeps giving, it exposed me to a new generation of fans,' Lundquist said.

At one point in the film as Happy Gilmore approached the first tee, Verne as the announcer placed his hand over the microphone so nobody could hear him and said, 'Who the hell is Happy Gilmore?' That line has evolved into a cult classic, along with the film.

Rita Coolidge - Singer/ Songwriter

We had singer-songwriter Rita Coolidge scheduled to appear as a guest on *Profiles* in the spring of 2018. She was in New York City to promote her latest album release, *Safe in the Arms of Time*, about which Coolidge said: 'I've written so many songs assuming a role like an actor, but this time I got to write from experience. This is the best recorded album I've ever done. I'm extremely proud of it.' That's saying a lot when you look back at many of her most memorable hits which include: 'We're All Alone,' 'Higher and Higher' and 'I'd Rather Leave While I'm in Love.' All great tunes.

A few weeks before our scheduled interview, I attended Rita's performance at The Cutting Room in the heart of New York City. Prior to her going on stage, I asked Rita's manager Nelly if Rita would be singing one of my favorite songs of hers, 'All Time High', the theme from the James Bond film *Octopussy*. Nelly laughed and said, 'NO! Rita HATES that song.' Of course, during the interview, I had to ask Rita why. Rita explained, 'It was a rushed, thrown-together song for the movie. I felt like it was never finished completely.' Nevertheless, it still remains one of my favorite songs of hers. For years it had been rumored that Rita wrote the piano coda to Eric Clapton's mega-hit 'Layla'. According to Rita 'I never received any credit or royalties and basically, Eric stole the music from me.'

'When I first heard 'Layla' on the radio I immediately recognized the piano coda section that I wrote and had given to Eric on a small cassette previously.' So I asked Rita why she hadn't pursued getting what should have been hers, a share of royalties. 'I DID!' Rita exclaimed. 'I contacted Eric's record company and they told me I didn't have enough money to fight in court, and they were right.'

In 2016 Rita released her autobiography, titled *Delta Lady*. In the book, Rita eloquently wrote: 'Sometimes the path is surrounded by rainbows, and sometimes it's buried in mud.' Two years prior, Rita's family experienced a horrible tragedy when her sister Priscilla was shot and killed by her husband. Who then turned the gun on himself. 'It deeply affected every part of my life,' Rita said.

No interview with Rita Coolidge would be complete without asking her about her turbulent marriage to Kris Kristofferson, whom she originally met at LAX Airport. When I asked Rita about Kris' heavy drinking she laughed and said: 'Yes, he arrived late and stoned to our 1974 wedding in Malibu. My parents never drank alcohol, but they did that day.'

Rita and Kris divorced in 1978, but they did have a beautiful daughter together, Casey Coolidge Kristofferson, who has made them grandparents three times. Rita mentioned: 'Today we're all good friends and family.'

When I reflect back on my interview with the two-time Grammy Award winner I found Rita to be charming, candid, refined and honest. And above all - still beautiful.

Felicia Collins - Guitarist

I was excited to have guitarist Felicia Collins as a guest on *Profiles*, which we did in the summer of 2018. I had been watching Felicia for 23 years as the guitarist and vocalist in the CBS Orchestra on the *Late Show with David Letterman*. It was a job she held for the show's over two-decade run.

The last *Letterman* show was on May 20th, 2015. 'Nothing will be as good for me as a musician,' Felicia said of her time on the show. In the weeks and months after the show ended many of its cast members experienced an extensive mourning period, Collins recalled: 'I just felt like there's nowhere to go after that. I was so depressed for months. I couldn't watch television, I couldn't talk to people.' Felicia credits her mom for eventually coming out of this post-*Letterman* malaise. 'My mother told me "get out there, you can't just look like you just dropped off the face of the earth." '

Felicia Collins grew up in Albany New York. At 12 years old she spotted and purchased her first guitar from an Albany pawn shop. 'It cost thirty-six dollars… but it might as well been thirty-six hundred dollars. It meant everything to me. When I got home, I proudly played it for my mom,' Felicia reminisced. 'After listening, my mom said, "Sounds kind of tinny." I laughed and responded, "It's an ELECTRIC guitar, Mom - I need an amplifier." ' The next day, the two headed back to that same Albany pawn shop and purchased a small cameo amplifier for twenty-one dollars. With guitar and amplifier in hand, Collins taught herself how to play the guitar. Today, she owns a little over one hundred guitars.

After spending her college years honing her skills, Collins headed for the Big Apple and eventually found work touring with Cindy Lauper, the Thompson Twins, and Al Jarreau. When she wasn't touring, she was in the recording studio with the likes of Whitney Houston, George Clinton, Ashford and Simpson, Chaka Khan, and Aretha Franklin. Then one day the phone rang; it was Paul Shaffer, who wanted Felicia as his lead guitarist for the then upstart CBS Orchestra. 'At first I wasn't sure if I should take the job,' Collins recalled. 'I asked Paul Schaffer if I could have a few days to think about it. I think Paul was surprised that I didn't immediately jump on the opportunity. Paul told me that would be ok, but added, "Don't take too long, we have to get this thing going." I didn't - I called Paul the following week and took the job, thank goodness.'

Fast forward twenty years as Collins was coming out of her post *Late Show* malaise, she received another career-changing call from Paul Schaffer, who was about to put together 'Paul Schaffer and the World's Most Dangerous Band', which would include many of the old CBS Orchestra members, and of course, he wanted Felicia as his lead guitarist. She accepted, and today she's back touring the world with Paul and the band.

Before the interview ended, I had to ask Felicia about her signature dreadlocks that extend nearly five feet long and reach down to her calves. Grinning ear to ear, she said: 'I let mother nature do my hair.'

From the Projects to *Profiles*

Irene Cara - Singer, Songwriter

In the spring of 2005, singer, songwriter, and actress Irene Cara was booked as a guest on *Profiles*. In 1980, Irene had catapulted to stardom with her role as Coco Hernandez in the hit movie *Fame*. She recorded the film's title song 'Fame', which evolved into a number one hit on the charts. Cara was born in the Bronx, New York City. By age five she began to play the piano by ear, then studied music, acting and dance seriously, and at age thirteen, she appeared on Johnny Carson's *The Tonight Show*, singing in Spanish. Cara grew up in a musical family. 'My dad was part of a big merengue band in the 50s. They brought the merengue to this country. They had the first big merengue hit on the top 40 Latin charts. Today, the merengue is a staple in Latin music,' Cara said.

Irene went on to record her first record by age eight. 'I did a Spanish album; that was my first album, that was my first record as a solo artist, everything was in Spanish and it was done by a very prominent Latin label. I was the little princess of the South Bronx.'

By the time she got her big break in *Fame*, in a way, she was already a show business veteran. 'A lot of people don't like to think that. They like to think a certain project makes you. I got a lot of flak for that in my late teens. I would tell the truth of the years that I put in before that and the work I'd done as a child and teenage actress in television with projects like *Roots* and various movies. They didn't want to hear it, they felt I was coming off like the little veteran brat. I wasn't trying to, I was just mainly being honest about my life and career. However, when my break came in *Fame* I was ready for it,' Cara said.

In 1980, Cara made Academy Award history by becoming the only performer ever to sing two Academy nominated songs, 'Fame' and 'Out There On My Own', in one evening at the Oscars. Cara laughed, and remembered, 'We did it like a medley. The producers and directors did a great job with it, they arranged it that way, it was a big thrill.'

With her performance in the classic film *Fame*, Irene inspired and motivated a generation of young people to become involved in the performing arts. 'I wasn't aware of what it had become at the time. I've been as far away as England and have heard schools in Liverpool that have opened up in the performing arts. So many of my fans tell me from all over the country and the world that they've become actors, choreographers, directors, dancers, and professionals in the entertainment industry because of the inspiration they garnered through that film,' Cara reflected.

In 1984, Cara once again returned to the Oscars, this time for co-writing and recording the hit song 'Flashdance – What A Feeling' from the hit movie *Flashdance*. She won the Academy Award that year for Best Original Song and a Grammy Award for Best Female Pop Vocal Performance.

Reflecting back on her career, Cara said: 'Seems like it was only yesterday. Time keeps moving forward and I feel like it all happened last week. Time moves so fast.'

Today Irene lives in Florida, performs occasionally and spends a great deal of her time as a music producer helping upcoming artists.

Dick Cavett - Talk Show Host

When I learned that we had booked legendary talk show host Dick Cavett for *Profiles* in the spring of 2006, I was excited, to say the least. I had always looked up to him as the prototype of what a talk show host should be: literate and intelligent. From 1969 through 1975, *The Dick Cavett Show* ran opposite NBC's *The Tonight Show Starring Johnny Carson*. Although the two shared many of the same guests, Mr. Cavett's intelligent approach to comedy appealed to a legion of fans and viewers to keep the show running for several years despite the competition from Carson's show.

Without a doubt, Mr. Cavett set the standard for quality conversation on television. His show was one of the few talk shows that were showcasing the rock stars of the time. 'When I had Mick Jagger of the Rolling Stones on, I laughingly asked him if he could imagine doing this when he's 60; when you're 30, 60 is the same as a hundred. Mick said quite cooly, "easily!" He's done and is still doing just that,' Cavett said.

One of his favorite rock stars featured on his show was Janis Joplin, who appeared five times. 'She was wonderful and she loved coming on. Maybe she was part of the reason other rock people came on and I became the home of the rock people without actually ever intending to. Another thing I can confess now - I was NOT as interested in their music as them,' Cavett lamented.

The day after the now famous Woodstock Festival in August 1969, Dick invited the 'Jefferson Airplanes', Joni Mitchell, David Crosby and Stephen Stills to the show. Today, it's referred to as 'The Woodstock Show'. Cavett remembered, 'I know that show has kind of a cult following. At the time I didn't think it was such a good idea the day after Woodstock, kind of an anticlimax. During that episode, Stephen Stills raised his left leg and said: "I still have the mud on my boots." That mud, wouldn't you love to be able to sell that on eBay today,' Cavett laughed.

In the early 70s, Dick had Sly Stone as a guest. 'To me, he was just a guy who didn't like to talk very much. Watching it recently, after people have said that must have been your most excruciating interview ever... No, it wasn't. Reflecting back, I think he was in charge, I think he knows what he's doing. He's not saying much but he gets a laugh, he doesn't mistime anything, you can't be stoned to the gills and do that, there was a method to his madness,' said Cavett.

The night John Lennon and Yoko Ono were guests on the show, Dick asked Yoko: 'You've been called the dragon lady that brought the Beatles apart...' Lennon stopped Dick mid-sentence and snapped, 'Please give her credit for all the nice music that George made and Ringo made and I've made since we've broken up, if she did it then that's the result.' Cavett nodded and said, 'I guess that's true.'

Reflecting back on having John Lennon and later George Harrison as guests Cavett said: 'I remember thinking these guys are so funny and such great entertainers and they're both so interesting with depth, [if it wasn't for the interview] you never would have seen it otherwise.'

I asked Mr. Cavett about his early beginnings. 'You grew up in Nebraska and so did Johnny Carson?' 'I thought you had to, to be a talk show host. I knew Carson out there, I met him, he was doing a magic show in the basement of a church. Probably getting thirty-five dollars. My friends and I went to see him, he introduced us from the stage and we felt like we were on the *Ed Sullivan Show*. He was very nice to us,' Cavett remembered.

During the interview with Dick Cavett, I clearly remember thinking of myself, *Thank you, Mr. Cavett, for making me feel like I'm not totally over my head.*

He was cordial, charming and interesting throughout our forty-minute interview. Afterwards, we posed for a series of publicity photos, during which I leaned towards him and said: 'You've always been one of my role models and one of the reasons I became a talk show host. I've always aspired to produce quality conversation like you've always done.' Dick smiled, propping an arm on my shoulder as we prepared for the next photo and said: 'Mickey, you're on my IN List.'

Misty Copeland – Prima Ballerina / Principal Dancer

We recently had ballerina Misty Copeland as a guest on *Profiles*. In 2015, Misty made history by becoming the first African-American woman promoted to principal in the 75-year history of the American Ballet Theatre. Misty said: 'This is for the little brown girls, and that everything I've gone through will hopefully make it better for them.'

Immediately, I realized that Misty took her responsibility as a role model extremely seriously. 'For years I was told that I didn't have the right body type to be a professional ballerina.

That was their way of saying that I was the wrong color,' said Copeland.

Misty's path to ballet stardom was certainly an unlikely one. For a period of time, as a child, Misty, along with her five siblings and her mother, was living in a motel, just trying to survive. At 13 years old, Misty was introduced to ballet at a local Boys and Girls Club at their gymnasium. She immediately took to the art form and was told by her teacher that she was a prodigy and that her goal should be to get to the American Ballet Theatre.

'Back then, I didn't even know what a prodigy was,' Misty laughed. Still, she worked diligently at her craft. In 1997, she won the Los Angeles Music Center Spotlight Award as the best dancer in Southern California. Three years later, she became a member of the American Ballet Theatre's Studio Company.

Ballet dancers are both athletes and artists. I asked Misty, of the two, which one she considered herself more of. Without hesitation, Misty responded: 'I consider myself as an artist.'

At 29 years old, she was given the opportunity to perform the principal role in Stravinsky's *The Firebird*, a tremendous opportunity for her career. During the first performance, Misty fractured her tibia in six places and needed immediate major surgery. 'Did you think at that point your career might be over?' I asked pensively. Misty shook her head, 'At first I was concerned about all of the people I felt I'd be letting down, but as far as returning, I knew I'd make it back.'

Misty was also eager to share her thoughts and emotions about her friend and mentor Raven Wilkinson, who was the first African-American woman to dance for a major classical ballet company. Wilkinson broke the color barrier in 1955. Misty recalled: 'The first time I saw Raven Wilkinson dancing in a video, it changed my life.' The two would become close friends. In fact, up until her death in 2018, Raven would call Misty before every one of her performances to say: 'May I be the wind at your back.'

Today, Misty is carrying the torch for countless minority children throughout the world. 'I think that my purpose is to bring people in, to make them feel that they belong and hopefully make it easier for them,' Copeland said.

I really liked Misty; she was one of the few celebrities who took the time upon entering our studio set to go up to every member of our crew to introduce herself and shake their hands. It was an impressive entrance, and won over my crew members with ease! She was cordial, pleasant and extremely polished.

In 2014, Misty released her *New York Times* best-selling autobiography titled *Life in Motion: An Unlikely Ballerina*. The following year, she was named one of the '100 Most Influential People in the World' by *Time* magazine. Without a doubt, Misty Copeland is a pioneer, a groundbreaker, a role model and, most importantly, an inspiration.

Aaron Neville - Singer

In 2010, I had the privilege of having singer Aaron Neville as a guest on *Profiles*. He was 70 years old at the time but didn't look a day over 30. His career began in the mid-1960s when he released his first hit, 'Tell It Like It Is'. He's also been a key member of the legendary Neville Brothers Band for over forty years. In the mid-1980s Aaron teamed up with Linda Ronstadt for a series of duets. The collaboration produced three consecutive mega-hits, two number one hits, and multiple Grammy awards.

Aaron grew up and lived in New Orleans until Katrina devastated the city in 2005. 'I've been back to New Orleans but I haven't been in my home since the hurricane struck,' Neville said. He was on the road performing and watched what transpired on television. 'I get sad passing all the old neighborhoods; some people are coming back and some of them are never coming back because they have nothing to come back to.' At the time of our interview, he was living in New York City.

Aaron's beautiful falsetto voice has often been called 'the only voice like it on the planet.' I asked Aaron, 'There's an incredible contrast between how you sound and how you look. You don't expect angelic sounds like you've been producing to come out of a muscular six foot, two hundred and thirty-pound guy that looks like a linebacker. Did you always have this beautiful falsetto voice, or is this something you had to acquire over time?' Aaron laughed and said: 'I always had the voice, but the body I had to work at. Me and my wife workout every morning.'

I then asked Aaron to explain his interpretation of the legendary New Orleans sound. He explained: 'It's gumbo, it's a mixture. My brothers always refer to it as the Caribbean island that's stuck to the United States, and the musical influences that create the New Orleans sound come from many different places. Not only is the music a form of gumbo, so is the food in New Orleans."

As Aaron sat across from me, I couldn't help but notice the array of tattoos on his face, chest, and arms. He explained that he got his first tattoo at fifteen years old. 'What do all the tattoos represent for you?' I asked. Aaron laughed and said: 'Just ink, they're like wearing a chain.' I responded by asking Aaron if he had any advice that he could share with today's young people regarding tattoos. 'Yeah - they don't come off. They're there for the duration. You better be sure before you do it,' Neville laughed.

Neville's first major hit single 'Tell It Like It Is' was released on a small New Orleans label called Par-Lo. The song topped *Billboard's* R&B chart for five weeks in 1967, and then reached number two on the *Billboard* Hot 100, right behind The Monkees' 'I'm A Believer'. It sold over one million copies and was awarded a gold record. I had read somewhere regarding the success of 'Tell It Like It Is' that Aaron never received his share of the royalties from the record. 'Back in those days, that was not uncommon in the music business. Eventually, the label went bankrupt.' 'Are you at all bitter about not getting properly compensated for your hit song?' I asked Aaron. 'Not really, the song gave me national exposure, that otherwise may have taken many more years to achieve. It's hard to put a price on that,' Neville said.

Aaron finally returned to New Orleans for the first time since Katrina in 2008 for the city's Jazz Fest, to perform with his brothers, The Neville Brothers Band, who closed the seven day festival.

At the beginning of the interview, Aaron looked up at me and said: 'I feel like I've already known you.' That made me feel like we were forming a special bond and for sure a friendship. God-given talent aside, I found Aaron to be a kind and sensitive man. It was an honor meeting him and having him as a guest on the show.

Mary Wilson – Singer

In the summer of 2007, Mary Wilson of the world famous group The Supremes was scheduled as a guest on *Profiles*. I had always loved The Supremes' music and I had been following them throughout the 1960s and 1970s. At the time of the interview, Mary was in her early sixties, beautiful as ever and impeccably dressed.

The Supremes were a female singing group and the premier act of Motown Records during the 1960s. In fact, they evolved into America's most successful vocal group by charting twelve number one singles on *Billboard* Hot 100 charts.

I started off by asking Mary, 'Besides the Supremes' enormous success as a vocal group, were you aware back then that your style and glamour made you role models for millions of young African-American girls?' 'Let's look at it socially,' she began, 'what the world was like, and even more so what America was like in the 60s. Back then, black was not beautiful, it was becoming beautiful. I'm one of those who grew up drinking out of the colored water fountains. That's what was going on socially, so for three little black girls in the 60s to dare to dream what was, back then, an impossible dream… and we did that - Florence, Diane and I did make our dreams come true.'

Before I could get another question in, Wilson went on to say: 'We did something that had almost nothing to do with singing. I mean socially, we were there in that movement and we helped to change that face or the faces of black people to the world.'

In 1986, Mary released her *New York Times* bestselling autobiography titled *Dreamgirl of Supreme Faith* which at that time became the most successful rock 'n' roll autobiography ever. Interestingly, Mary had a difficult time getting the book published. 'It took a long time to sell it. The publishers did not want the book, they wanted a book based on Diana Ross. I kept telling them that this book is about The Supremes, and Diana Ross is one of the three and it's about her as well, but it's about all of the Supremes,' Wilson recalled.

I had to ask Mary, 'Are we ever going to see a Supremes reunion tour?' Mary snapped right back: 'Are we? Ask Diana. It's all up to her. If she decides to do it, we'll do it. But they will have to pay me my third or more. They can't come at me like they did before, as if I was never there. I was a Supreme. In the past, they didn't want to pay me. It was all about the money.'

In the beginning, The Supremes struggled to come up with a hit; in fact, Wilson said she thought it may never happen for them. In 1964, the songwriting team of Holland-Dozier-Holland presented them with the song 'Where Did Our Love Go?' 'Initially, we hated it. We all felt that this song would never be a hit,' Wilson recalled. 'Holland-Dozier-Holland assured us that this would be a number one hit for us. They were right and we were wrong.' That song opened up the floodgates for the group. They would go on to chart four other number one hits in 1964 - 'Baby Love', 'Come See About Me', 'Stop! In the Name of Love', and 'Back in My Arms Again' - breaking the record for the most number one hits by an American group in one year, with five.

When I asked Mary how she felt about her legacy as a Supreme, she smiled and said: 'I have really done a lot to keep the Supremes history alive and intact, clean and brilliant, and I plan on continuing to do just that!'

From the Projects to *Profiles*

Ron Darling – Former Major League Pitcher

In April of 2019 former major league baseball pitcher Ron Darling was a guest on *Profiles*. Ron was a key member of the 1986 World Champion New York Mets. I was always a big fan of Ron's, and loved the way he pitched throughout his career. In fact, I said to him during our interview, 'I always felt opposing hitters were guessing up at the plate against you.'

During the interview I mentioned that the first three batters he faced in the major leagues were Joe Morgan, Pete Rose and Mike Schmidt. All are in the Baseball Hall of Fame with the exception of Pete Rose who has been excluded from the hall because he had bet on games, while as a player and later as a coach. Ron got the trio out, one, two, three. 'Better lucky than good,' Ron said with a giggle. Nevertheless, it was a great way to start off a major league career. Darling remembered, 'That was one of the biggest thrills of my life because my entire family was there to support me.'

I then proceeded to ask Ron about the infamous 1986 New York Mets. 'The '86 Mets were a tremendous team beating the Boston Red Sox in the World Series that year; however, do you feel that group should have gone on to accomplish greater things?' Ron snapped right back, 'Absolutely, I felt we should have been in at least two more World Series; for a number of reasons it never happened but we did have one of the greatest seasons of all time.' We also discussed the much written about cocaine use among a few key members of the '86 Mets, which Ron candidly admitted didn't help with the longevity of success for the squad.

In the 1986 World Series Ron was exceptional in games one and four, not so good in game seven. He lasted only four innings before being taken out of the game. I asked Ron, 'What happened in game seven?' 'I think I over-thought the process. In doing so, I lost the confidence and edge that I had in games one and four. Boston was a great team and I was thinking that it's not easy beating a team of that caliber three times in a series. Reflecting back, I think I talked myself out of doing better that night,' Darling explained. The Mets rallied and beat Boston in game seven, becoming World Champions. In spite of Ron's shortcomings in game seven, he was a key part of that accomplishment.

Literally two weeks after our interview Ron was all over the news having been diagnosed with thyroid cancer. I was shocked; he looked so great for our interview, certainly not like someone with a serious illness. Ron had surgery immediately, and the prognosis for a full recovery appears to be excellent.

After his retirement from the game on his birthday in 1995 Darling said he went cold turkey from the game of professional baseball. 'I went into a depression upon leaving the game, in fact, I couldn't even watch a game on television for a few years,' Darling said. Then out of the blue, he got a call from a friend to work as a color analyst up in the booth. 'I got the same adrenalin rush as a broadcaster as I did as a player. I was elated to be back in the game,' Darling remembered. Since 2006, Ron's been working New York Mets games up in the booth on the SNY Network with former teammate Keith Hernandez and Gary Cohen and loving every minute of it.

Graham Nash – Singer/Songwriter

In the spring of 2017, we had booked English singer and songwriter Graham Nash on the show. I was a big fan of Graham's since his days as a member of the Hollies back in the 60s, and I was excited having the opportunity to discuss his many musical accolades with him. He was internationally known for his beautiful tenor voice as a member of the English pop group the Hollies and the folk-rock supergroup Crosby, Stills and Nash. Graham was inducted into the Rock 'n' Roll Hall of Fame as a member of both bands, Crosby, Stills and Nash in 1997 and the Hollies in 2010. A trio at first, Crosby, Stills and Nash later became a quartet with the addition of Neil Young.

I started out by asking Graham how his life changed after meeting David Crosby and Stephen Stills. 'In 1968 when I first sang with David and Stephen and we immediately found that vocal blend. I realized at that moment I would have to go back to England and leave the Hollies, my family and my friends. I then headed for Los Angeles to follow that vocal sound that David, Stephen and myself had created,' Nash remembered.

'At what point did you realize that you guys had something really special?' I asked Graham. 'About a minute into the very first song we ever sang together. We were having dinner at Joni Mitchell's house. After dinner we headed for the living room, and began singing. I had my harmony part down quickly and that vocal blend was born in a minute,' Nash said.

Back in August of 1969, Crosby, Stills and Nash were among the headlining acts to appear at the infamous Woodstock Music Festival which was billed as '3 Days of Peace and Music'. I asked Graham, 'What was it like performing in front of those 400,000 people at Woodstock?' 'It was an amazing event! When we were arriving in a helicopter Crosby jokingly said that it was like flying over an encampment of the Macedonian Army. Looking out of the helicopter window at all of those fires and mud along with the thousands and thousands of people is something I'll never forget,' recalled Nash.

Graham then leaned forward in his chair. 'Mickey, a month before the show there was supposed to be twenty thousand people, then three weeks before a hundred thousand, and two weeks before two hundred thousand, it kept getting bigger and bigger. But I'll tell you this, if every person that told me they were at Woodstock were actually there, the planet would have tilted,' Nash said with a big laugh.

I had to ask Graham the current status of Crosby, Stills, Nash and Young: will we ever see them perform together again? With a pensive look on his face Graham responded, 'In terms of Crosby, Stills, Nash and Young, I believe David Crosby's negative comments about Neil's girlfriend Darryl Hannah really upset Neil. When Neil Young is upset, he means what he says and if he says the group won't play together again, then that's it!'

According to Webster, a lasting impression is defined as continuing to exist or have an effect for a long time. Each of the celebrities that I have written about in this chapter have certainly left a lasting impression on me.

Oscar Wilde once said: 'Be yourself, everyone else is taken.' Reflecting back, what I remember most about each of them was that they were all extremely unique, one of a kind. They each had their own special personalities, their own individual journeys towards success. All demonstrated laser focus, with a determined drive to succeed, and each had a unique ability to persevere while overcoming numerous obstacles throughout their lives. Looking back, I feel honored that they were all willing to share their stories and life with me on *Profiles*.

On the set of Profiles in Times Square NYC waiting for our
next guest to arrive (2018)

Here are some of the guests I have had the pleasure to host....

**(Left to right) Singer Chubby Checker and Dog The Bounty Hunter
(Duane Chapman) (2012)**

With Actor Robert Wagner (2017)

With Kenny G (2017)

With Actress Susan Lucci (2017)

(Left to Right) Actress Ming Na and Actor Lou Diamond Phillips (2009)

With Singer Meat Loaf (2017)

With Singer Don McLean (2017)

With Actress Tia Carrere (2014)

Chatting with Singer Bill Medley after our interview (2016)

With Deepak Chopra (2018)

Welcoming Ballerina Misty Copeland to Profiles (2019)

With Singer Tom Jones (1980)

With Actor Danny Aiello at Patsy's Restaurant in Times Square, NYC

With Singer Davy Jones of The Monkees (2006)

With Heavyweight Boxing Champ George Foreman (2007)

With La Toya Jackson (2011)

With Singer Engelbert Humperdink (2016)

With Darryl McDaniels (Run DMC) and Hollywood Casting Director Sheila Jaffe (2015)

With Singer Tony Orlando (2018)

With Rock n' Roll Hall of Fame Inductee Darlene Love (2019)

(L-R) Artist LeRoy Neiman and Muhammad Ali (2001)

With The Greatest Muhammad Ali (2001)

With Country Legend Charlie Daniels (2017)

With Actress and Dancer Leslie Caron (2010)

(L-R)With Artist LeRoy Neiman, Mickey Burns, and Football Great Joe Namath

With Legendary Comedian Joan Rivers

Chapter 9
Some Days Are Just Really Special

Muhammad Ali

One of our early *Profiles* episodes featured artist Le Roy Neiman, who was known for his brilliantly colored, expressionist paintings and screen prints of athletes, musicians and sporting events. He was probably the most popular living artist in the United States before his passing in June 2012.

I really liked Le Roy, whom I became friendly with in the years following our *Profiles* interview with him in 2000. He was a great storyteller and I loved hearing about the many tales he experienced while working on features for *Playboy* magazine titled 'Man At His Leisure', where he would paint illustrations that chronicled his travels to exotic locations around the world. Every once in a while, our office would receive a call from Mr. Neiman's publicist Gail Parenteau asking us to come to Le Roy's studio, which was located on Central Park West, to video document a special event.

One such call came in February of 2001. Gail explained that Muhammad Ali would be spending a day at the studio signing nearly a thousand serigraphs of Le Roy Neiman's 'Muhammad Ali – Athlete Of The Century' painting. Gail wanted to know if we would be interested in documenting the event for Le Roy. We accepted immediately!

On the day of the event we arrived early at Mr. Neiman's studio to set up a couple of cameras along with the lighting. We wanted to get everything just right for 'The Greatest'. Muhammad walked into the studio around noon. He immediately walked around the studio shaking hands with the few people lucky enough to be present. The champ wasn't very verbal but his eyes were alert and full of charm. When Muhammad Ali walked into the room, it was his. We all knew that we were in the presence of greatness.

Muhammad didn't appear to be in any rush to begin his serigraph signings; instead, he decided to entertain us with a series of magic tricks, which he was really good at. He performed for approximately twenty minutes with a big smile on his face. Afterwards, I said: 'That was great champ', and Ali then turned towards me making a fist and putting it up against my chin and said: 'Did you call me a chump?' I quickly replied, 'No, I said champ.' He laughed while walking over to the main table to begin his serigraph signings.

After signing approximately three hundred serigraphs, Muhammad needed a break and asked Mr. Neiman if he could have some paper and charcoals because he said he'd like to do some drawing. Mr. Neiman quickly set the champ up with everything he needed. For the next hour or so Muhammad Ali, totally focused, attempted to create his masterpiece as I stood right next to him the entire time. He was drawing a night scene with a ship entering what appeared to be a harbor. Every so often, Ali would glance up at me and say, 'Mickey, what color do you think I should use for this?' I happily offered my best opinion, while reminding Ali that I was no Picasso. He found that amusing and kept asking for my opinion nonetheless.

When he was finished, you could see that he was extremely proud of his creation. He signed his drawing and handed it to Mr. Neiman. I then asked Le Roy, 'What are your plans for Muhammad's drawing?' He leaned over to me and whispered in my ear, 'This one's going into my private collection.' I often wonder where that drawing is today. Watching Ali create it was as special as it gets.

After his drawing break Ali went back to signing the remaining serigraphs for the rest of the afternoon. Towards the end Ali appeared to be getting a bit tired, but who wouldn't after signing one thousand serigraphs? However, before leaving Mr.

Neiman's studio Ali made sure to give everyone in the room a photo opportunity. When it was my turn, he thanked me for my help with his drawing and I thanked him for a day that I'll always cherish.

Joe Namath

A few years later, Gail Parenteau called us once again. This time she said: 'Le Roy has Joe Namath coming into the studio to do signing for his 1969 New York Jets Limited Edition Serigraph and he would like you to come in and video document the day.' We accepted immediately.

When we arrived at Mr. Neiman's studio Joe was already there, looking dapper in a navy blue turtleneck and a nicely tailored sports coat. Le Roy introduced us to Joe and then led us into the big studio for the serigraph signings.

Signing serigraphs for hours on end can get somewhat boring. So while Joe was signing one serigraph after another, he and I would talk continuously about life and sports. We talked in depth about his childhood growing up in Beaver Falls, Pennsylvania, where he was a three sport standout in high school. After graduation in 1961, Joe received offers from several major league baseball teams, including the New York Yankees, Indians, Reds, Pirates and Phillies. So I asked Joe why he passed on professional baseball. 'I really wanted to sign with the Pirates, my idol was Roberto Clemente. However, I decided to stay with football because my mother wanted me to get a college education,' Joe explained.

In 1962, Namath enrolled at the University of Alabama and played football under legendary coach Bear Bryant, who often said that Namath was one of the greatest athletes that he ever coached. Namath led Alabama to a National Championship in 1964.

As Joe continued to sign away at the pile of serigraphs we talked a great deal about Super Bowl III, a game which secured his legendary status. I asked Joe, 'Why did you tell the press three days before that Super Bowl that you guaranteed a New York Jets victory?' With a pensive look on his face Joe said: 'To be honest, I was responding to a heckler. I was also tired of hearing that the AFL didn't measure up to the NFL. In my heart, I sincerely felt we were going to win that game.' Joe backed up his statement, as he led the New York Jets to a 16 to 7 win over the heavily favorite Baltimore Colts while becoming Super Bowl III's Most Valuable Player.

As the day was winding down I asked Joe what time his flight back to his home in Florida was. He laughed and said: 'Actually, I have a private jet waiting for me at LaGuardia Airport. When I leave here I'll call the captain and tell him to start warming up the plane, I'm hoping to be home for dinner.' I wondered quietly to myself, do all Super Bowl MVPs live this way?

Before he left Mr. Neiman's studio, Joe made time to take photos with everyone present. As he was walking out of the door he thanked us for our work and company. I then shook his hand and thanked him for a special day that I'll never forget.

Tom Jones

In the mid 1980s, when I was starting to get my foot in the door at Fox News in New York City, my mentor and golf partner, former Fox anchor Bill McCreary, asked me if I'd like to accompany him to see singer Tom Jones in concert at Westbury Music Fair in Long Island. I had been to Westbury many times for various concerts, which included Peter Allen, Engelbert Humperdinck and Smokey Robinson. It was a great place to watch a concert. The round stage revolved and there really wasn't a bad seat in the room.

I was always a huge fan of Tom Jones and loved his many hits including 'It's Not Unusual', 'Delilah' and 'I'll Never Fall In Love Again', just to mention a few. I was also an avid watcher of his television series, *This Is Tom Jones*, which was broadcast internationally from 1969 through 1971. So when Bill made his offer to attend Tom's upcoming concert at Westbury, I graciously accepted.

As the date for the concert grew closer, Bill said to me: 'By the way, we're going backstage to meet Tom in his dressing room prior to the concert.' I immediately thought to myself, 'This is going to be great, what a treat!' On the day of the concert I drove out to Queens to pick Bill up at his house and from there we headed out to the Westbury Music Fair. As soon as we arrived, security quickly escorted us directly to Tom's dressing room. Security knocked on the door, which had in bold lettering 'Tom Jones' with a big star below his name. Within seconds the door opened, and to our surprise, there was Tom Jones welcoming us in to join him.

My first impression of Tom was that he was a bit shy and reserved, a far cry from his on-stage persona. Nonetheless, he was friendly and accommodating. We sat down and chatted with Tom for approximately twenty minutes, and every once in a while Tom would get up and peek out of the door to see if the room was filling up. It was obvious that he was excited and ready to get out there to perform.

Tom had established the reputation of being one of the hardest working performers in show business; he worked all of the time. During our conversation, I asked Tom: 'Why do you work so hard, are you at all concerned that your workload might eventually take its toll on you and your voice?' Without hesitation Tom said: 'I'm smart enough to realize that nothing lasts forever. I'm so lucky to be where I am today and as long as people continue to fill up those seats out there, I plan to cherish every minute of performing for them.' Tom took a few seconds to gather his thoughts and then added, 'I know the day will come when people won't come out to hear me sing anymore; until that day comes I'm giving it everything I have.'

It was almost show time. Before we said our goodbyes we posed for several photos with Tom and then headed to our seats - which were front row - that Tom had provided for us. We were so close to Tom during his performance, it was like he was performing for us in our living room. A truly special night.

In 2006, he was knighted by Queen Elizabeth II for his service to music. In 2020, Tom will be turning eighty years old. His concerts continue to sell out throughout the world. His voice, which has been described as full-throated and robust, continues to be kind to him.

Chapter 10
Fifteen Glancing Thoughts

As the years continue to roll by since we began producing *Profiles*, there is always something specific that remains with me for almost all of our 500 episodes. Sometimes it's a comment, a point or a gesture from the guest. It stays etched it my memory for one reason or another. When I reflect back to specific interviews, I refer to these instances as 'glancing thoughts.'

1. Harry Wayne Casey – singer and songwriter. In May of 2016, we had Harry Wayne Casey as a guest on *Profiles*. Best known as KC, the founder and lead singer of KC and The Sunshine Band, he has written and recorded numerous chart-topping hits such as 'That's The Way I Like It', 'Get Down Tonight', 'I'm Your Boogie Man' and 'Boogie Shoes' to mention a few. However, KC admitted he felt he never got the respect and accolades as a songwriter that he feels he should have gotten. 'I'm like the Rodney Dangerfield of songwriting, I never got any respect. My songs were no more simplistic than many of the songs written by Lennon and McCartney.'

2. Jesse Ventura - pro wrestler, actor, and former governor of Minnesota. During our *Profiles* interview in the spring of 2017, I asked Jesse about his role as Blain in the 1987 classic film *Predator*. 'During the filming, the talk on the set was, who had the bigger arms: me or Arnold Schwarzenegger? One day, a producer measured both of our arms, and it turned out that mine were an inch bigger. Arnold had a fitness trailer on the set and every morning before filming he'd go there and work out. I'd find out what time he would be arriving and get there a half hour before him. It really drove Arnold crazy when he realized that my arms were a bit bigger,' Ventura recalled.

3. Bill Medley - singer, songwriter, and one half of The Righteous Brothers, Bill was a guest in the fall of 2017. I had read that Bill formed a close relationship with Elvis, and during our interview, I asked him to describe their friendship. 'We met when we were both performing in Las Vegas,' Medley reflected. 'He was starring in the main room and I was performing in the lounge. I think we hit it off because our personalities were very similar; we were both kind of shy and reserved off stage. We had long talks nearly every day during our time in Las Vegas together. We became good friends.' We also discussed The Righteous Brothers' first hit in 1964, 'You've Lost That Lovin' Feeling', which was produced by Phil Spector. The length of that record was around four minutes, almost twice as long as most records of that time. 'We were concerned that, because of the song's length, disc jockeys might decide not to play it, but that never happened. Instead, they ended up playing it every time they had to go to the bathroom, and often referred to 'You've Lost That Lovin' Feeling' as The Potty Song,' said Medley.

4. Bruce Campbell - actor/movie-maker. Known as the undisputed king of the modern B-movie, Bruce, along with his high school buddy Sam Raimi, raised 350,000 dollars to make the first *Evil Dead* movie in 1983. The film first gained notoriety in England where it became the best selling video of 1983. Six years later the duo was able to raise ten times as much cash for the sequel *Evil Dead 2*. Bruce was a guest on *Profiles* in the summer of 2017.

I asked Bruce, 'Today, with advances in technology, can movies be made cheaper?' With a big smile on his face, Bruce responded: 'I theorize you can make a movie today for ten grand. You buy two good computers, an HD camera for 500 bucks. Music editing and sound effects software is readily available.

When you're done you put the project on a thumb drive and you can take it to your local theatre and put it in their digital projector.'

What about the hard work required to be a filmmaker? Campbell laughed and said: 'The new technology doesn't weed out the slackers. Now slackers can make movies. Slackers were never in the film business before because the process of movie making was really hard.'

5. Tanya Tucker - country singer. Tanya joined us as a guest on *Profiles* in the summer of 2009. Often referred to as the original bad girl of country music, during our interview I asked Tanya about her reputation as a party girl and being promiscuous. 'The truth is, yes, I partied a lot, especially on the road. It can get very lonely on the road. I had a fan base that followed me all over the country. Many of them evolved into good friends. After shows, we would all go out for drinks. But I was never promiscuous, I just liked having fun and enjoying myself. However, reflecting back, those rumors of promiscuity did make for great press,' Tanya said with a giggle.

6. Little Anthony – singer. His vocal group, Little Anthony and The Imperials, was inducted into the Rock 'n' Roll Hall of Fame in 2009. Anthony joined us on *Profiles* in the fall of 2017. A native of New York City, I asked Anthony what it was like growing up in Brooklyn. Anthony said: 'I was a terrible student in high school. One year, I missed sixty days and had to go to summer school. One hot July day, I was sitting in the back of the classroom with my small transistor radio close to my ear. All of a sudden, my song, 'Tears On My Pillow', began to play. I got so excited, I got up and walked out of the school. I never returned. I thought to myself, who needs school? I'm a star now!'

7. Charlie Daniels – country singer. Charlie was a guest on *Profiles* for the second time in the winter of 2015. Best known for being the founder and frontman for The Charlie Daniels

Band, and for his mega-hit 'The Devil Went Down To Georgia', Charlie has spent most of the last five decades on the road performing all over the country and the world. I asked Charlie about the perils of being on the road so frequently, to which he answered: 'The road is not for everyone. I've seen it devastate many musicians. However, I love it. I love waking up in a different motel parking lot each and every morning.'

8. Sally Kellerman – actress. During our *Profiles* interview with actress Sally in the spring of 2011, she mentioned that she had once hired Harrison Ford to build her a daybed hutch in her den during his early struggling acting days. Sally recalled: 'One day while he was working in the den, he told me he just got a part in some *Star Wars* film. At the time I thought to myself, it's probably some bad B-movie production. Boy, was I wrong! In retrospect, it's a good thing he made it in the movies. The daybed hutch he built for me was terrible, it ended up about a foot shorter than it was supposed to be.' Harrison Ford retired from carpentry the following year.

9. Stacy Keach – actor. In the fall of 2015, actor Stacy joined me as a guest on *Profiles*. I had been a big fan and was an avid watcher of his popular television series *Mike Hammer* back in the 80s. In 1984, Stacy was arrested by London police at Heathrow Airport for possession of cocaine, to which he pleaded guilty and served months at Reading Prison for. So I asked Stacy, what happened? 'As I was going through customs, the agent, as he was going through my carry-on, noticed that I had two cans of shaving cream. One can had a screw off bottom - that's where I kept the goods. When the agent asked me why I was carrying two cans of shaving cream, I knew I was in trouble. I retrospect, I really think I wanted to get caught,' Keach reflected. In his autobiography, *All In All: An Actor's Life On And Off The Stage*, the renowned actor candidly reflected on his life and career. His memoir received a Prism Award, an award given to projects helping people who are in the grips of addiction.

10. Bobby Rydell - singer and teen idol. We had Bobby on *Profiles* in April of 2016 while he was in New York City to celebrate his 75th birthday. In 2012, Bobby underwent a double organ transplant to replace his liver and a kidney, in his hometown of Philadelphia. During our interview, Bobby attributed his health problems to bouts of alcoholism, which escalated in 2003, after his wife of thirty-five years, Camille, passed away. 'I was trying to drown away my sorrows with booze. I couldn't even play a round of golf without having a quart of vodka in my golf bag. I was in bad shape,' Rydell recalled. Back in the 60s, Bobby was one of the original teen idols, along with Frankie Avalon and Fabian. When I asked Bobby what it was like being a teen idol, he laughed and said: 'Back in the day, the women would throw me their room keys - today they throw me Depends!'

11. Lou Diamond Phillips – actor. Hollywood leading man Lou Diamond Phillips, who was full of charm and personality, joined us on the set of *Profiles* in the fall of 2009. Since gaining attention with his portrayal of teen idol Richie Valens in the hit film *La Bamba*, which Phillips referred to as: 'catching lightning in a bottle', he would go on to star in over eighty films, including: *Young Guns, Courage Under Fire* and *Stand and Deliver*. Lou has built an impressive resume, not only in acting but also as a writer, producer and director.

During our interview Phillips said: 'There's a lot of guys that were around when I made *La Bamba* who weren't as fortunate as I was with their careers. And it's not a matter of talent or hard work, it's just the breaks sometimes.' After gathering his thoughts, Lou went on to say: 'It's a constant struggle to stay relevant in this business and to maintain the level of quality and exposure you need to stay on top. This is why I ventured into other facets of show business, including Broadway.'

Versatility has certainly been one of the keys to his success. In 1996, Phillips earned a Tony Award Nomination for his lead role in a revival of *The King And I*.

12. Sebastian Maniscalco – comedian. The man Jerry Seinfeld called 'my favorite comedian', Sebastian Maniscalco joined us as a guest on *Profiles* during the summer of 2011. Sebastian is one of the few comedians to have been able to sell out five consecutive shows at Radio City Music Hall in New York City. As he walked onto the set, I would describe his demeanor as laid-back and cool. He was extremely relaxed and slouched down in the chair across from me as if he were a friend joining me in my living room.

I started the interview off by asking Sebastian: 'How did you originally acquire the comedy bug?' His response was, 'As a small kid I always enjoyed going in front of the class, giving a book report or presentation. However, I was never the class clown, I was very shy. But when I got on stage I felt very comfortable.' Sebastian credits the support of his family for much of his early success, especially his father. 'When Dad comes to a performance, he never sits down, he's always walking around the room looking at people's reactions while taking notes. He's like [having] a coach, he's my biggest critic but it's always good. I think he knows my act better than I do,' Maniscalco explained.

Since our interview, Maniscalco's career has blossomed and he has been as successful as any comedian could hope for. In fact, he was recently listed as one of Pollstar's 30 highest-grossing performers in the world.

13. Burt Young – actor. In the spring of 2006 I was excited to have veteran actor Burt Young as a guest on *Profiles*. Although his acting resume was filled with five decades of accomplished work, he is best known for his role as Rocky Balboa's brother-in-law and best friend Paulie Pennino in the *Rocky* film series. That role earned Young an Oscar nomination for Best Supporting Actor in 1976.

I asked Burt: 'Sequels have seldom been as successful as the original, what do you attribute to the continued success of the *Rocky* franchise?' 'Because it has a background of action, but more importantly, it's really about the common man. He doesn't even have to win, he gets knocked down time and time again and always gets up. He's every man who tries and refuses to give up,' Young explained.

Burt appeared in all of the first six *Rocky* films. However, he did not reprise his role in the 2015 film *Greed* with his character described as having died in 2012.

14. Mario Lopez – actor and entertainment journalist. In the summer of 2008 the popular Mario Lopez joined us. At the time he was starring on Broadway in the musical *A Chorus Line* in the role of Zach. Shortly thereafter, Mario began hosting the syndicated entertainment news magazine show *Extra*. Few people in show business are as versatile and productive as Lopez, which he credits to his fitness regime and lifestyle. He has long been recognized for having one of the hottest bodies in the business. Just prior to our interview he celebrated the release of his fitness book titled *Mario Lopez: Knockout Fitness*.

'Fitness has been a big part of my life for a long time. I grew up playing various sports and made many mistakes along the way regarding my fitness, especially with nutrition,' Lopez said. Mario was a championship wrestler in high school.

So I asked Mario: 'How does your fitness program differ from the many get fit quick programs out there?' 'Variety is the key; if you're not having fun you won't stick with it. My workouts are centered around having fun. Of course, you need discipline, sacrifice and consistency, however, my goal is to keep it interesting and to keep the muscles guessing,' explained Lopez. He went on to say, 'Good nutrition is a vital component to any successful fitness program.'

15. James 'Murr' Murray – comedian. In the fall of 2018 James 'Murr' Murray of the extremely popular *Impractical Jokers* joined us on *Profiles*. The *Jokers* have been making television audiences laugh till they cry and cringe in equal measure since 2011 on TruTV. The *Impractical Jokers* consist of four lifelong friends who hail from my hometown, Staten Island, New York.

I started off by asking Murr, 'What's been the key to the enormous success of the *Impractical Jokers*?' 'It's definitely our friendships growing up on Staten Island. We created a show that puts our friendships first, the format of the show is secondary,' Murray explained.

To illustrate how far the foursome have come, ten years earlier the group, then called The Tenderloins, performed a show in Manhattan and only two people showed up. 'We rented a theater in Manhattan that cost us sixty five dollars, only two people showed up paying five dollars each. So we ended up losing fifty five dollars,' Murray said, laughing.

Fast forward a decade, when the *Impractical Jokers* played to a sold out Madison Square Garden. Murray fondly remembered, 'When we were at the Garden I came out of the subway on Seventh Avenue; when I looked up at the gigantic marquee it read: "Impractical Jokers, Sold Out". Instantly, tears started streaming down my face. I couldn't help but to think back to that show ten years earlier when only two people showed up and how far we've come.'

Chapter 11
Things I've Learned Along The Way

Learning is a funny thing; it never stops as long as you're open to it. As far back as I can remember I've always had an insatiable appetite to learn new things, whether it be in my profession, my life or my hobbies. I remember my high school English teacher telling the class, 'If you learn one new word every day, just imagine what your vocabulary would be like in twenty years.' He was right, and that was some great advice. However, I also understand that it takes a disciplined thought process to accomplish things like that.

PASSION

A few years ago I had former NFL football great Herschel Walker as a guest on *Profiles*. When he walked onto the set I couldn't help but notice how physically fit he still looked after retiring from professional football in 1997. My first question to Herschel was, 'How do you stay so fit?' Without hesitation Walker responded, 'Every day I do a combination of approximately two thousand push-ups and sit-ups.' He went on to say, 'I learned this from my high school football coach who told me that every time a commercial came on the television, to get up and do push-ups and sit-ups instead of sitting like a couch potato.' Smiling, Herschel said, 'I took his advice and have been doing that exactly that ever since.' As the interview progressed, he began explaining his passion for fitness and it reminded me of one of my favorite quotes, 'If you are working on something that you really care about, you don't have to be pushed.'

INSPIRATION

During my years of interviewing accomplished guests, I've learned that they were all, in one way or another, inspired by someone else who in turn drove them towards success and even greatness. One definition of inspiration is 'a feeling of enthusiasm you get from someone or something that gives you new and creative ideas.' If something or someone is the inspiration for a particular project, work of art, or action, they are the source of the ideas in it or act as a model for it. For example, The Beatles acted as a model of inspiration for legions of bands that followed them.

When I reflect back on my twenty years of hosting *Profiles*, I think there was something about every guest that inspired me to some degree. Some guests for their talent and accomplishments, others for overcoming challenges, and many for making a difference.

PERSEVERANCE

One guest who especially inspired me was singer and songwriter Theresa Sareo who lives in New York City. Nine months to the day after 9/11 Theresa was waiting to cross a busy street at a Manhattan intersection when she was struck by an impaired driver in a Ford Explorer. She lost her entire right leg. Reflecting on the accident Sareo said: 'I could never have fathomed this morning was the end of my simple life, singing for a living, with a cozy little place in the city. In the blink of an eye, my life changed drastically and permanently.'

Within several months of her accident and painful rehabilitation, Theresa began volunteering with new trauma patients at Bellevue Hospital, where she had been a patient. According to Dr. H. Leon, former Trauma Chief at Bellevue Hospital, 'Theresa is an inspiration for a generation of people, myself included. The mettle of an individual cannot be judged when things are going well, only when things are not. She is way above the curve.'

After her accident Theresa never stopped singing and songwriting, while using her talents in a new and inspiring way. She's made frequent visits to Walter Reed Army Hospital to work with and perform for wounded soldiers returning from Iraq and Afghanistan. 'Today I use my music in hopes of inspiring humanitarianism, healing and communion,' Sareo said. Former First Lady of the United States Michelle Obama said of Sareo, 'Your example of service... shows that each of us can make a difference for those around us.'

CONTINUOUS LEARNING

In talking to all the guests we've had on *Profiles*, another common thread appeared: you are never too old to pursue new goals and passions. Personally, it drives me crazy when I hear people say, 'I'm way too old to try that.' That mind frame is ridiculous and I believe that age is just a number.

Singer and songwriter Graham Nash, who recently turned 77, said during his interview on *Profiles*, 'I get up every day with the intention of being creative, whether it be with my music, art, or photography.'

SELF-REINVENTION

When former *Profiles* guest George Foreman decided to make a comeback as a professional boxer at age 38, he said, 'Everybody thought I was crazy, especially my wife.' Foreman went on to say, 'All I kept hearing was, George you're way too old. All that negativity just served as motivation, I wanted to prove them all wrong.' And that's exactly what he did. On November 5, 1994 Foreman knocked out Michael Moorer in Las Vegas to win the World Heavyweight Championship at age 45.

When I decided to pursue a broadcasting career at age 40, just like it was with George Foreman, everyone told me, 'You're too old to get into broadcasting, you'll never get a job, it's a young man's game.' Just like George, I thought to myself, 'Oh yeah, I'll show them.' I believed in my abilities, and the hard work that I knew was ahead of me to achieve success in broadcasting was welcomed.

A MISCONCEPTION

One thing that's always bothered me within the broadcasting industry is that executive producers and station managers are constantly searching for shows that attract the younger eighteen-to-thirty-year-old demographic. I've been saying for years that the eighteen-to-thirty-year-old viewing audience is virtually non-existent in television today. This age group is not watching traditional television; instead they are on their on iPads, iPhones and computers. So who's watching television these days? According to a 2008 study conducted by Magna Global, the average age of the television viewer was 50 years old. Two years later, it was 52 years old. I can only imagine what it is today, but I would venture to guess the average age would be somewhere in the high 50s.

I've always felt that much of the success of *Profiles* can be attributed to the fact that we produced a series showcasing celebrities who our viewers watched on television and grew up with. For us, it was a simple formula: understand your viewing demographics and create programming that they would like to see.

I think the rest of the television industry is finally getting it. For an indication of this, you need to look no further than to see what companies and products are currently advertising on television. If you take a closer look, what you'll find are commercials for luxury automobiles, tons of pharmaceuticals for everything from high blood pressure to stroke prevention, and erectile dysfunction medication - all of which are most likely of little interest to the eighteen-to-thirty-year-old viewing demographic.

OUR QUEST FOR PERFECTION

I've also learned during my years of hosting *Profiles* that no one is perfect, especially those people we put on pedestals. No matter how successful or great they are, they're still human. They make mistakes and have problems like everyone else. For example, while being interviewed on *Profiles*, entertainer Tony Orlando said that cocaine abuse cost him a marriage and a television series. Singer Bobby Rydell openly admitted that alcohol abuse nearly killed him. He was saved by a double organ transplant. Singer Isaac Hayes said that he wore sunglasses all the time to hide his insecurities. Singer B.J. Thomas used so many drugs in the 1960s that he candidly admitted that he has little memory of his performances back then. Singer Melba Moore, after a bitter divorce, had to fight her way back after bankruptcy. Entertainer Ben Vereen was hit as a pedestrian by two cars on the same day. Professional billiards player Jeanette 'The Black Widow' Lee became a world champion while suffering from severe Scoliosis. Renowned public speaker and author Bonnie St. John became a Paralympics medalist after losing her leg as a child. Ronnie Milsap became a Grammy Award winning country singer in spite of becoming blind as a young boy. Matt Roloff became a television star at four feet tall. At the height of his career actor Kevin Sorbo (Hercules) suffered a stroke at 39 years old. Guitar god Tony Iommi cut off the tip of his finger at work before the success of Black Sabbath. Singer Bill Medley lost his singing voice completely at the height of his career and had to re-learn to sing.

These are just some of the examples of guests that I've had on *Profiles* who made mistakes, had to overcome personal problems and in some cases physical obstacles in order to continue their careers at the highest levels.

We often hear the term perfectionism, which is defined as a personality trait characterized by a person's striving for flawlessness, setting high performance standards, accompanied by critical self-evaluations and concerns regarding others' evaluations. In my younger years, I believed that in order to achieve your goals and dreams you had to be perfect. It took me many years to realize that nothing we create is perfect, because all humans are flawed to some extent.

LEARNING FROM MISTAKES

When I was a high school basketball coach back in the 1970s, my team had a couple of undefeated seasons. One newspaper headline read *McKee High School – Perfect at 20 – 0*. We may have had an unblemished record, but we were far from perfect. What we were was talented, determined, hard working and disciplined, not perfect. The belief is that to be perfect means that the end result is flawless. When I reflect back on our undefeated seasons, I firmly believe that it was our imperfections that were an essential ingredient to our success. We knew we had imperfections and worked hard every day to eliminate them. In the end we were not perfect; however, we were very good.

I would tell my team all the time, 'Don't worry about making mistakes; instead, focus on your role and be the best you can be.' I clearly remember other coaches screaming at their players after they made mistakes. I'm sure for those players the experience was embarrassing and humiliating. I did just the opposite. My father told me as a young boy, 'When you make a mistake on the field, never make a fuss and bring attention to it. Instead, quickly move on stone faced and no one will even realize that you've made a mistake.' He was right!

When one of my players made a mistake, I would just smile at them and then point to my temple. This meant: make a mental note of the mistake and try to eliminate that kind of mistake moving forward. Usually the player would smile back and point to his temple, which meant: I got it, Coach. No yelling, no embarrassment, just a subtle way of bringing attention to expected mistakes. In my opinion, when players feared embarrassment from their mistakes, they were more likely to make them, and less likely to make good plays. Back then, I called it 'Hearing footsteps from the sidelines.'

DOING THE BEST YOU CAN

I take a similar approach today with my production team on *Profiles*. On the set we all make mistakes from time to time. I consistently tell my team, 'If you make a mistake, correct it and move on as quickly as possible.' As a production team we always strive to be as good as we can be. However, sometimes I just have to say, 'Let's go', my point being that if we waited for everything to be exactly perfect, we would probably never finish another episode.

I've been playing golf most of my life, which would equate to hundreds of rounds. With each outing, I've made numerous mistakes, such as hitting the ball out of bounds or missing an easy three foot putt. However, with each round I also hit a couple of shots perfectly, exactly the way I visualize the trajectory and result of the shot to be. Interestingly, after the round I seldom remember the bad shots, and always remember the good ones.

Life is trial and error, and so is golf. When I'm playing golf I'm doing something I'm passionate about. To think I could play a round of golf flawlessly would be ridiculous. Instead, I try to learn from my mistakes and cherish my successes. Basketball legend Michael Jordan recently said: 'I've failed over and over again in my life and that is why I succeed.' I continue to remind myself, every time I go out to play golf, that there are no mistakes, only lessons I need to master.

CHANGE IS GOOD

Sometimes change is good. I also realize that change is hard because our brains are wired to do the same thing over and over regardless of the activity. Change can be challenging, but it helps us grow and offers new perspectives.

For example, over our twenty years of producing *Profiles*, every five years or so, we moved to a new location for our set. We started out producing the show from the stage of the Music Hall at the Snug Harbor Cultural Center. When we learned that the Music Hall would be undergoing renovations, we moved to

Ashford and Simpson's restaurant known as the Sugar Bar located on the upper west side of Manhattan. Today, we produce *Profiles* from Times Square at the historic Algonquin Hotel.

With each move to a new location there was an expected amount of resistance. Some liked being in the same place and sticking to their comfort zone. However, what we learned was that with each new move the show got better. The new environments challenged our creativity and enhanced our focus. Each change made us more flexible and adaptable. Change is good when welcomed.

OVERCOMING FAILURE

Failure is part of every journey: learn from your failures and keep moving forward. I remember reading that the *American Idol* television series, which became the most successful television series of all time, didn't start off that way. *American Idol* originated in the United Kingdom and when its producers attempted to bring the series to the United States, every cable network originally passed on the show. Eventually, Fox reluctantly took a chance on *American Idol* and placed the program on its network as a summer replacement series. The rest, as they say, is history. The point here is, although you may be getting many 'no's along your journey, it only takes one 'yes' to make your dreams and goals come true.

HARD WORK

Actor Kevin Hart recently said: 'Everybody wants to be famous, but nobody wants to do the work.' And American inventor Thomas Edison said: 'Genius is 1 percent inspiration and 99 percent perspiration.' Webster simply defines hard work as 'a great deal of effort.' Most people feel that hard work is the only key to achieving our goals in life. I tend to agree.

One of the by-products of hard work is sacrifice. What are you willing to sacrifice in order to reach your goals? In many cases sacrifices can impact family life, relationships and hobbies. However, I've learned that many of these sacrifices tend to be temporary: once you've given 110 percent in your quest to achieve specific goals and ultimately succeed, the sense of achievement acquired will only strengthen relationships.

So when Kevin Hart said: 'Everybody wants to be famous, but nobody wants to do the work', I disagree. I feel it's not that people are resistant to the hard work, but rather are hesitant to make the sacrifices that the hard work requires. My mother would often say to me: 'If it was easy, everyone would do it.' I think she was right. For me, motivation has always been the key to putting in the hard work. What's the pay off? For many, it's the money and career advancement. However, for me it's always been about the sense of achievement garnered after the hard work has been completed.

It's also important to surround yourself with people who are supportive and understanding in your quest to achieve goals that require a great deal of hard work and sacrifice. How often have you heard extremely successful people credit their children, friends and spouses for the support they offered during their arduous journey? Never forget, it takes a village to be successful.

AND FINALLY

What I've learned the most after producing five hundred episodes of *Profiles* is that I still have a lot to learn!

Chapter 12
Those We've Lost

I've been hosting *Profiles* for nearly twenty years. What an honor it's been to interview so many celebrities, many of whom are considered icons in their field. I'm reminded that no one is immortal, as this list of episodes features many great people who were lost. For example, Dr. Maya Angelou, Joan Rivers, Davy Jones, Ernest Borgnine, Eli Wallach, David Brenner, Al Martino, Carol Channing, Teddy Pendergrass, Frank Vincent, Isaac Hayes, Chuck Barris, and Peter Tork, just to mention a few. When I think back, I feel a great deal of gratitude having had these opportunities.

To honor some of those who have left us, I'd like to share my thoughts of sitting down with them on *Profiles*.

Teddy Pendergrass - Singer

A native of Philadelphia, Teddy dropped out of school in the eleventh grade to enter the music business. In 1970 he made his name as the lead singer of Harold Melvin and the Blues Notes with his raspy baritone voice.

During an interview on *Profiles*, saxophonist Kenny G said that he once witnessed Teddy in concert. 'Teddy Pendergrass was unbelievable, the audience was 90% women and he had every one of them swooning... I never saw anything like that,' he lamented.

Teddy's rising career was suspended in March of 1982 after a near-fatal car crash that left him paralyzed from the chest down.

We were able to schedule our interview with Teddy in March of 2009 if we were willing to drive from New York City down New Jersey Turnpike to his home in the suburbs of Philadelphia. Without hesitation, we booked a time and date for the interview and began preparations for the trip.

The day of the interview was a beautiful and sunny day. After an hour and a half drive, we pulled up to Teddy's house, on a nice tree-lined street in southwest Philly. I knocked on the door and was greeted by Teddy's assistant, who led me and my crew to the living room for set-up. About 40 minutes later, Teddy appeared, rolling in on his wheelchair and wearing a baseball cap. I can't imagine how difficult it must have been for Pendergrass, both physically and mentally, to be confined to that wheelchair after years of knocking them dead on stage.

Before we started rolling I complimented him on his home. Teddy laughed and said: 'You know, I never really made much money in music; being part of Harold Melvin and the Blues Notes was great, but he wasn't the best in paying his musicians.' He then explained: 'After my accident, whatever money I did have I invested in real estate, and lucky for me, I did so at a time that made me a lot of money.'

I then asked Teddy, 'What was it like being a key member of Harold Melvin and the Blue Notes?' 'It was a great hard-working band and I loved being a part of it all. However, Harold always had a problem paying the guys, that was not his strong suit,' Pendergrass said, with a big grin on his face.

The interview went well: we talked about his life, his music and of course his 1982 car accident which would change his life forever. Amazingly, he continued his successful solo career from his wheelchair through the late 80s until announcing his retirement in 2007. Teddy died from respiratory failure in January 2010.

Ernest Borgnine – Actor

We had award-winning actor Ernest Borgnine as a guest on *Profiles* in 2008, when he was 91 years old. When he arrived on set I was surprised how great he looked at 91 - barrel-chested, full of energy and sharp as a tack.

One of my first questions was, 'How do you stay so mentally sharp at 91?' His answer: 'Everyday when I wake up I do crossword puzzles... exercise for the mind.' Makes sense to me!

After a stint in the Navy during World War II, he ventured into acting through the encouragement of his mother who told him: 'You're not that good at anything else, so why not give acting a try.' He did, and in 1955 won the Oscar for Best Actor for his performance in the film *Marty*. In 1962, he was offered to play the title character in a new television sitcom, *McHale's Navy*. Ernie said he was reluctant at first, 'After all, I was a movie star. In those days, it was generally considered a career downturn when movie stars venture into television.'

One of the highlights of the interview for me was our discussion about his marriage in 1964 to singer Ethel Merman which lasted only 42 days. Ernest said that while they were on their honeymoon in Hawaii, he was constantly mobbed by fans of his sitcom, *McHale's Navy*, which was extremely popular at the time, and he was the star of the show. According to Borgnine, 'Ethel threw a jealous fit regarding the lack of attention she was experiencing in comparison.' Ernie went on to say, 'This upset me so much that I decided to end the marriage right there.' They divorced after just 42 days of marriage. Merman's description of the marriage in her autobiography was a solitary blank page.

Ernie continued acting well into his 90s, and in 2009 he appeared in the last episode of the long-running medical series *ER*. His performance garnered an Emmy nomination for Outstanding Guest Actor in a Drama Series. Mr. Borgnine died of kidney failure on July 8, 2012. He was 95 years old.

Eli Wallach – Actor

The Good, the Bad and the Ugly! Who could forget Eli Wallach's role as Tuco (The Ugly) opposite Clint Eastwood in Sergio Leone's classic spaghetti western? However, Mr. Wallach was a huge star way before that film; he was one of the greatest character actors ever to appear on stage and screen. He showed his versatility in 1961 when he co-starred with Marilyn Monroe, Montgomery Clift, and Clark Gable in *The Misfits*, which turned out to be Monroe's and Gable's last film before their deaths.

To say Eli Wallach had a prolific acting career would be an understatement. He was an acting chameleon who worked in film and on stage for over seven decades. As I waited for Mr. Wallach to arrive for our interview, visions of his films were dancing wildly in my thoughts. As he entered the set, I knew I was about to be in the company of acting royalty.

'Eli Wallach, welcome to *Profiles*'… we shook hands and off we went. We discussed his upbringing in Red Hook, Brooklyn. His parents, both Jewish immigrants, owned Bertha's Candy Store in Red Hook. Eli decided to attend the University of Texas in Austin to study acting, which was an unlikely journey for a kid from Brooklyn. Wallach said he learned to ride horses while in Texas, which was a necessary skill for his role in *The Good, the Bad, and the Ugly*. Wallach said: 'Sergio Leone nearly killed me twice during the filming, once on a horse with my hands held behind my back, and the other when I was almost decapitated by a passing train.'

While at the University of Texas he performed in a play with fellow students that included Ann Sheridan and Walter Cronkite. Wallach mentioned that Cronkite wanted to be an actor badly. 'Needless to say, Cronkite eventually found his niche,' Wallach said with a big grin on his face.

It was a fabulous interview. Afterwards, as we took photos and chatted around the set, it was time to say goodbye. As I walked Eli to the door he turned to me and said: 'Mickey, take a walk with me.' I replied: 'It would be my honor.' So here I was walking up Broadway near 72nd Street with this amazing man when I noticed that he was carrying something in a plastic bag. I said 'Mr. Wallach, what are you carrying in the bag?' He laughed and said: 'A pair of shoes that I'm taking up to the cobbler for repair.' Kidding him, I responded: 'With all of your money, why not go down to Macy's and buy five new pairs?' That's when Eli got serious, stopped walking, turned to me and said: 'Mickey, I grew up in the Depression; back then we didn't buy new, we fixed old. It's something I've never been able to shake.'

I will never forget my day with Eli Wallach, who was 90 years old at the time. He passed away from natural causes in 2014 at the age of 98.

Chuck Barris – Host/Game Show Creator

I loved my interview with Chuck Barris, who became famous for hosting *The Gong Show* and creating *The Dating Game* and *The Newlywed Game* back in the 1960s.

Barris said that when he first had the idea of producing *The Gong Show* he originally scoured the country for great acts, but when reflecting back, admitted, 'I couldn't find any.' So instead Barris incorporated a parody concept with some of the worst acts in show business that he could find. It was an enormous national hit! As for the host of the show, Chuck tried out everyone in Hollywood, but said: 'No one got it, so I figured I'd host the show myself.' Chuck's jokey, bumbling personality was a perfect fit for the show.

I asked Chuck how he originally got into television before becoming head of daytime television at ABC. He explained with a laugh, 'I was applying to be a page at ABC but didn't know anyone. So I went to the library, found and listed the top five ABC executives on my resume as references.' Then with his hands waving in the air, he said: 'Mickey, it was the darndest thing, they never checked and shortly thereafter hired me as a page, I couldn't believe it.'

A little known Chuck Barris fact is that he wrote 'Palisades Park', which became a huge hit for Freddy 'Boom Boom' Cannon. 'Palisades Park' peaked at number three on the *Billboard* Hot 100 for two weeks in June of 1962.

So I asked Chuck: 'Was hearing 'Palisades Park' on the radio for the first time one of your biggest lifetime thrills?' Chuck responded with an emphatic, 'Yes!' He went on to explain, 'I was driving on the Westside Highway when I first heard it on the radio, I couldn't take it, I had to pull the car over and stop. It was one of the biggest thrills of my life.' Interestingly, Barris also wrote or co-wrote most of the music that appeared on his game shows.

I then asked Chuck why we didn't get more hit records from him. Barris explained: 'At the time, payola, which was pay-for-play, was haunting the music business. I was hired by ABC to be Dick Clark's watchdog. Executives told me that if I wanted to keep my job that I had to get out of the music business completely. I understood where they were coming from; however, that ended any aspirations I had to write more songs.'

At the end of the interview, I asked Chuck, as I do all of my guests, 'What do you hope your legacy will be?' His response: 'I'd like it to be written on my tombstone - Gonged At Last.' Barris died in March of 2017, and from what I've read, I believe he got his wish.

Dr. Maya Angelou – Poet/Author

Every once in a while we would book a guest for *Profiles* and I would immediately say to myself in a *Wayne's World* sort of way, 'I'm not worthy!' Such was the case when I learned I would be interviewing Dr. Maya Angelou.

While doing my research I learned that Dr. Angelou had published seven autobiographies, three books of essays, several books of poetry, and was credited with a list of plays, movies and television shows spanning over 50 years. She was also a civil rights activist and is considered one of America's greatest poets. Here I was, a kid from the South Beach Projects, now an adult, calling himself a television host, about to sit down with this American icon. Boy, was I in over my head!

The interview was to take place at the Schomburg Center for research in black culture located in Harlem, right around the corner from The Apollo Theater. Dr. Angelou was in attendance to receive an award and to share a few words with those in attendance, which she did eloquently.

It was time for our interview. My first question was, 'Do you realize how much you inspire people?'

Dr. Angelou responded, 'I'm very grateful; however, I'm evolving. I'm finding out that you can be a blessing or you can be a curse. If when your name is mentioned somebody says *Oh God!* then maybe you want to rethink how you're living your life.' I then wanted to ask Dr. Angelou about her versatility. During her life, she had worked as a cook, cable car operator, dancer, journalist, and actress, just to mention a few of her series of occupations.

She looked up and smiled at me and said, 'The truth is we don't understand talent. We don't understand electricity, we probably use one billionth percentage of what's available. If you are stupid you will ill-use me, if you're intelligent you'll use me for the furtherance of your field. I think talent is like that, we don't know what it is."

Before we totally got off the subject Dr. Angelou once again smiled at me and said, 'But I think every person is born with talent.' Once again, I thought to myself, does that include this wannabe TV host from the South Beach Projects?

I'm not sure if I was ever totally relaxed during the interview. The fact is, Dr. Maya Angelou can be a bit intimidating, with her abundant intellect, although I did my very best to hang in there with her. However, towards me, she was kind, charming and giving. I will always cherish my time with her, it was a total blessing.

One fact I learned during the interview, a fact that would go on to haunt me afterwards, was that Dr. Angelou was born on April 4th, 1928. April 4th is the same day that Dr. Martin Luther

King was assassinated. Dr. Angelou was extremely active in the civil rights movement and worked closely with Dr. King. After his death in 1968, Dr. Angelou would never again celebrate her birthday. It remained that way until her death on May 28, 2014. She was 86.

Isaac Hayes – Singer/MusicProducer

Early on in the *Profiles* series, around 2000, we booked musical icon Isaac Hayes for the show. We had unsuccessfully failed at booking him for over a year and a half. Finally, his schedule had a window for an interview with us - I was excited!

In the early 70s, Hayes was one of the top acts in the music business. Additionally, 'Black Moses' was highly respected by his peers as well as executives throughout the music industry. Isaac had been a major player in the success of Stax Records, where he produced records for Sam & Dave, Carla Thomas, and Otis Redding before venturing into a solo career after the success of his haunting theme to the mega-hit film *Shaft*.

I found Isaac to be the ultimate gentleman; he exuded no airs of superstardom, which he had experienced for decades. He was mild-mannered and pleasant.

First question: 'So Isaac, what's up with the sunglasses, I don't think I've ever seen you not wearing them?' With a pensive look on his face, Isaac replied: 'I'm really insecure and shy, and the sunglasses always served as a buffer between me and the audience. It felt as if I was hiding behind them.' When I asked Isaac about his childhood he was extremely candid. 'I grew up very poor and was raised by my grandmother. My clothes were so tattered that I was embarrassed, that's the reason I dropped out of high school.'

At the 1972 Academy Awards ceremony, Isaac's song 'Theme From Shaft' was nominated for Best Original Song, which ultimately won him an Oscar. The night of the awards, Isaac escorted his grandmother as his date to the Oscar ceremony. He never forgot the sacrifices she had made in raising him and wanted to share and honor her on the biggest day of his life.

In 2006, Isaac suffered a stroke and later recovered. Ten days before his 66th birthday, Hayes was found unresponsive in his home in the suburbs of Memphis. The cause of death was listed as a recurrence of a stroke.

Frank Vincent – Actor

It was in the spring of 2006. At the time *The Sopranos* was the most popular series on television and we were going to have one of its stars, Frank Vincent, as a guest on *Profiles*.

Often cast as a gangster, he played prominent roles in several films for director Martin Scorsese that included *Raging Bull* (1980), *Goodfellas* (1990) and *Casino* (1995). However, before making it big as an actor, Vincent made his livelihood as a musician. In the 1960s he was known as one of the better drummers in the New York, New Jersey area. Interestingly, during the 60s, Vincent had a three-piece band along with then-guitarist Joe Pesci. The band was called the Aristocats, and he and Pesci successfully played up and down the Jersey Shore. Then, as Vincent explains: 'I get a cease and desist letter from the Walt Disney Corporation to stop using that name.'

In 1970 Disney released the animated comedy film *The Aristocats*, a title that had been carefully copyrighted. When they found out a band in New Jersey was using the name, out came the cease and desist letter. As Vincent remembers it: 'I had this little band playing the Jersey Shore. Besides the fact that we had no money, what was I going to do, take on Disney? So we quickly changed our name.'

One night when they were playing down the Shore, a producer approached Vincent and Pesci and asked them if they would be interested in acting in a low budget gangster movie titled *The Death Collector*. Vincent remembers looking at Joe, then turning back to the producer and saying: 'Why not?' Thus, the acting careers of Joe Pesci and Frank Vincent were about to be launched. As it turned out Robert De Niro caught the film, and was impressed with both Vincent and Pesci. De Niro told Martin Scorsese about the duo, and the rest, as they say, is history.

Of his many roles, Vincent might be most famous for his role as Billy Batts in Scorsese's film *Goodfellas*. When I asked Frank about the lasting popularity of Billy Bates, he smiled and said: 'When people stop me on the street they always say, *Go home and get your shine box*. I could buy a new Mercedes if I had a buck for every time that happened.' I then asked Frank about his role as Phil Leotardo in the award-winning HBO series *The Sopranos*. He quickly responded: 'I originally went in to audition for the pilot with David Chase. I went to the audition with Tony Sirico and Dominic Chianese, they both got hired and I didn't. In retrospect, David felt that he didn't want to hire me because *Goodfellas* was too popular and the character of Billy Bates was too well known to put into that mix.'

Two years later David Chase called Vincent back in and gave him the role of Phil Leotardo. In September 2017, Vincent suffered a heart attack. He underwent open heart surgery and died shortly thereafter. He was 80 years old.

David Brenner – Comedian

In the spring of 2006, I was getting ready to interview comedy legend David Brenner on *Profiles*. I was well aware that after making his national television debut in 1971 on *The Tonight Show with Johnny Carson* he would go on to become the show's most frequent guest, with a record 158 appearances. I wasn't aware that he was as polished as any other celebrity I had ever interviewed on *Profiles*. He was relaxed, charming, and with every question I asked David he had an interesting story to go along with his perfectly timed response. I was immediately able to see why David was Johnny Carson's favorite guest, so much so that he even served as Carson's guest host 75 times. So going in I knew I would be interviewing a master of talk show discussions. However, he never made me feel like he was slumming. Instead, he treated his *Profiles* interview like another *Tonight Show* appearance. I will never forget the respect he offered me.

During my research, I noticed that David was among Comedy Central's 100 Greatest Stand-Ups of All Time. So I started off the interview by asking David: 'Are you as passionate about comedy today as you were when you first entered the business?' His response surprised me: 'I don't think I've ever been passionate about comedy. I got into this as a lark; I was a documentary writer, producer, and director. I stopped that for one year. I'd always been funny so I got up on stage as a lark, enough to get through a year. At the end of that year, I thought no one is going to believe that I'm a comedian and that I did it. So I decided to do one television show and then quit comedy, it turned out to be the *Tonight Show* and I had ten thousand dollars' worth of job offers the next day. I hit the motherlode.'

At one point in his career, Brenner had appeared more often on major television talk shows than any other entertainer. So I asked David: 'As a true veteran of comedy, do you still aspire to get better with time?' Brenner responded: 'You learn something every time you're on stage, whether it's a good show or a bad show you learn something, and if you don't realize that you're missing out on something.' Brenner built a reputation of being 'the king of observational comedy'. When I asked him about that title, he laughed and said, 'Comedy is tragedy with the passing of time.' Which brought us to 9/11. Brenner said: 'After 9/11 I worked that night even though the headlines said *Las Vegas Goes Dark*.' David couldn't understand why people were in the audience that night until after the show people started rushing up to the stage to thank him for giving them some relief. And he did it with humor. 'People were so depressed that this was their outlet, it was their medicine,' Brenner concluded.

David Brenner died on March 15, 2014, at age 78, from pancreatic cancer.

From the Projects to *Profiles*

<u>Lesley Gore – Singer</u>

In the fall of 2005 singer Lesley Gore was booked as a guest on *Profiles*. Like many baby boomers I grew up listening to her hits such as 'Judy's Turn To Cry', 'You Don't Own Me' and her signature classic 'It's My Party', for which she was nominated for a Grammy Award. With over two dozen hits, Lesley certainly helped create the soundtrack to the sixties.

In 1963 when Lesley recorded 'It's My Party' she was a junior in high school in Englewood, New Jersey. The song sold over one million copies and was quickly certified as a gold record. According to Lesley: 'It was a time when the record companies were first beginning to understand that they had a youth market, and they were taking full advantage of that.'

When I reminded Lesley that I still hear her songs playing on the radio all the time, she responded, 'The fact of the matter is in the top twenty cities on markets, their top radio station is usually an Oldies Station.' Many critics still consider many of her hits as classics: 'They've been around a whole lot longer than I expected them to, over 40 years I think you can call them classics. I can tell you that when we recorded them we really never expected that they would be played 40 years later,' Gore said.

Most of Gore's hits were produced by Quincy Jones, who was an A&R executive at Mercury Records. Gore remembers: 'He heard some demos of mine, called me one Thursday when I came home from school - I was all about 16 years old - and he made me an offer I couldn't refuse.' Back then, Quincy was using innovative techniques such as double-tracked vocals and intricate backup vocals and chorus. According to Lesley, 'In 1963 and 1964 double voicing was illegal by the union. We used to leave the recording studio, say goodnight, and 30 minutes later Quincy, Phil Ramone and I would return to the studio after the union member left and put the double voice in.'

As she and Quincy continued to crank out hit after hit, it marked the beginning of a time when fans would show up on her front lawn in Tenafly, New Jersey. Gore said: 'It was a different time, my mother would go out and give them cookies.' One thing Lesley seldom got credit for was her songwriting prowess. In 1980 she earned an Oscar nomination for co-writing 'Out Here On My Own' for the film *Fame* with her brother Michael. And in 1996 she co-wrote the song 'My Secret Love' for the film *Grace of My Heart*.

I found Lesley to be kind, personable and extremely candid about her career. She had been working on a memoir and Broadway play based on her life when she died of lung cancer in February 2015, at 68 years old.

Joan Rivers – Comedian

We had comedian Joan Rivers on *Profiles* twice, the first in 2009, and again in 2012. Both interviews were both memorable and special. Joan had carved out a show business career that few could rival. She had found enormous success as a comedian, writer, actress, producer, television host, and businesswoman. I was excited to have the opportunity to sit down with her.

I started off by asking Joan: 'At what point in your life did you realize that you were funny and that you could make a career out of it?' Joan responded: 'I knew I was funny and could make people laugh by the time I was in the third grade. Not like a class clown but witty. I knew I was verbally very funny.'

Joan grew up in Brooklyn, New York and attended Barnard College where she graduated Phi Beta Kappa while studying anthropology. 'I found anthropology fascinating, it still fascinates me,' Rivers said. She went on to say, 'To go into an area and dig down and find entire amalgamations and figure out what was happening then, it was a wonderful thing.'

I then asked Joan, had she not entered show business would have she stayed with anthropology? Joan laughed and said: 'Yes, if I could have brought along a hair and makeup girl.' Joan's big break came in 1965 when she was booked as a guest on *The Tonight Show starring Johnny Carson*. 'I got on *The Tonight Show* because Bill Cosby was a friend of mine, and the night before he was on the comic was so bad Bill told Johnny, Joan couldn't do worse. So I got on by mistake,' Joan remembered.

As versatile as Joan's career has been I wondered if this was all part of her master plan. Joan responded: 'I have no plan. I look at people with great awe and admiration that have plans. But that's show business, you have 30 balloons in the air and you pray that one will come down and be the lucky one.' Before she hit it big, Joan served as a comedy writer for other comedians and television shows. I asked Joan if writing for others helped her in the beginning to becoming a better comedian. Joan said: 'Writing for others was wonderful because it takes you one step away. You could also see if I took a joke and improved it or made it worse. It was all a learning process.'

Rivers was open about her multiple cosmetic surgeries during our second interview. In 2009, she had written a book on the topic titled: *Men Are Stupid And They Like Big Boobs: A Woman's Guide to Beauty Through Plastic Surgery*. In fact, Joan was one of the few celebrities honest enough to admit what she had done through plastic surgery to keep looking so fabulous.

So I asked Joan about her plastic surgery motto, which is: 'Better a new face coming out of an old car than an old face coming out of a new car.' Joan replied: 'No question about it, you can leave the car at the curb but the face goes into the party with you.'

My next question to Joan was: 'How do you respond to women who want to be loved for who they are as opposed to some artificially enhanced version of themselves?' Without hesitation, Joan responded: 'They're idiots, but if that's their wish then do it. If you think you're fabulous as you are, how lucky are you.'

At this point in the interview, I was interested to get Joan's take on her numerous plastic surgery procedures, so I asked her: 'You've had your eyes done, nose done, facelift, liposuction, breast reduction, botox, and a tummy tuck?' Before I could finish my question, Joan said: 'Nothing is going to change you, you're still going to look like you if you have a good doctor. Plastic surgery has made me happier to be me because for my age I look better and cleaner. It also got me on *Nip/Tuck* and it got me this book.'

In 2017, *Rolling Stone* magazine ranked Joan sixth on its list of the 50 Best Stand-Up Comics of All Time.

Joan Rivers died on September 4th, 2014, from complications after undergoing a minor treat procedure at an outpatient clinic in New York City.

Carol Channing - Actress

Carol's performances as the gold-digging Lorelei Lee in *Gentlemen Prefer Blondes* and the matchmaker Dolly Gallagher Levi in *Hello, Dolly!* made a Broadway legend. She once said: 'Performing is the only excuse for my existence.' Her talent and longevity certainly made her one of the most recognizable actresses in the theater world.

Carol was a guest on *Profiles* in the spring of 2005. She was 84 years old at the time, still charming and full of life. She was wearing a beautiful red leather jacket over a black turtleneck, and she looked stunning. My first question to Carol was: 'What's been your favorite stage performance?' Without hesitation Carol responded: 'Honestly, it's the show I'm in at the moment. It's like being in love, you can't remember being in love with anyone else.'

We then discussed her recent marriage to Harry, her childhood sweetheart, after a seventy-year separation. 'Harry had a beautiful sixty-year marriage, and I had a miserable forty-two-year marriage, and we were both widowed,' Carol said. Harry escorted Carol to the interview and sat in the background throughout. I responded to Carol by saying: 'The two of you look like a billboard for happiness.' She almost jumped out of her chair and said: 'I'm afraid of that; Bette Davis and Gary Merrill got married and at the time she gave the formula for a happy marriage, and by the time the magazine article came out they were divorced,' Carol said with a big smile.

After getting married Carol and Harry settled on his farm in Modesto, California. 'I've traveled all my life, so really this is the first home I've ever had and it's fabulous,' Carol said.

When I asked Carol about her over five thousand performances on Broadway in *Hello, Dolly!* she smiled and said: 'It never got boring, I just kept learning, it's such a privilege to keep doing the same thing, Finally, I got it right on the last performance.'

At one point in our interview, Carol appeared to be surprised with the amount of research that I had compiled regarding her life and career and said: 'Mickey, you really did your research. Many interviewers sometimes ask: *Now Carol, what is it that you do?*' I was flattered to be complimented by Carol Channing; however, to be in any way unprepared for an interview with the great Broadway star would have been disrespectful.

Carol Channing passed away at 97 years old on January 15, 2019, in her home in Rancho Mirage, California. The following evening Broadway theaters dimmed their marquees in honor of the Broadway legend.

Al Martino – Singer/Actor

One of our early *Profiles* interviews was with singer and actor Al Martino, who had experienced enormous success as a singer between the early 1950s and mid-1970s. During that period Martino was often described as 'one of the great Italian American pop crooners.' One of his biggest hits was 'Spanish Eyes', written by Bert Kaempfert. The song reached number eight on the pop charts and earned Martino several gold and platinum discs for sales. During the interview, it was evident that he was extremely proud of his Italian heritage. His parents were immigrants from Abruzzo, Italy. Once in the States, they established a construction business. Growing up, Al worked in the business alongside his brothers, Pasquale and Frank. Martino recalled: 'I used to get up at 5am and go to a construction site. I would work at that until 5pm then I'd go home and get dressed up to go sing at a nightclub, which usually got me home at 2am. My father would constantly tease me by saying that between 2am and 5am he was thinking about getting me a milk route.'

In 1972, Al's career was re-energized by his starring role as singer Johnny Fontane in *The Godfather*. Reflecting back Martino said, 'I loved being part of the iconic film, it added another dimension to my career. It was like the icing on the cake.' I asked Martino how many takes it took to complete the scene where Marlon Brando slaps him across the face. 'Just once, thank God,' Martino laughed.

The Godfather went on to become the highest-grossing film of 1972 and for a period of time was the highest-grossing film ever made. The famous wedding scene was filmed on Todt Hill on Staten Island. Many of my friends and former teachers worked as extras within the wedding scenes. Looking fabulous, Al Martino playing Johnny Fontaine in his white suit was a key part of the wedding scene. He also sang the film's title song, 'The Love Theme From The Godfather'.

The interview was arranged by my friend, professional singer Carl Thomas, who has been a long time friend of Mr. Martino. This might have been our third or fourth *Profiles* episode. We were far from established at that point in time. Some weeks after the interview Carl gave me a call and said: 'Mickey, to tell you the truth, Al was extremely wary about doing the interview, I had to convince him to do it. Afterward, Al said he was glad he did it. In fact, he said it was one of the best interviews he'd ever had. That's high praise from someone who's not known for giving it; congratulations.'

On October 13th, 2009, Al Martino died from a heart attack in his childhood home in Springfield, Pennsylvania, just six days after his 82nd birthday.

Peter Tork – Musician/Actor

One of our early *Profiles* episodes featured singer, musician, and actor Peter Tork, a member of the world-famous rock group The

Monkees. Back in the late 60s Peter, along with fellow Monkees Davy Jones, Mickey Dolenz, and Michael Nesmith, were the hottest things on the planet. The Monkees first invaded teen hearts in the 60s with their Emmy Award winning television series *The Monkees*.

At the time of the interview, Peter was touring the country with his new band Shoe Suede Blues. 'I always loved that era of music when Little Richard and Fats Domino were prominent. It was a magic time in the world when pop music, blues, rock 'n' roll, and soul music were all the same music,' Tork said.

Back in the early 60s Peter was part of the Greenwich Village scene in New York City, playing many of the coffee houses and clubs there. 'In 1965, I was walking down the street in the lower east side, and I got a higher calling that told me to leave New York, so I headed out west,' Tork said, adding: 'I landed in southern California at the end of June '65 and I signed the contract to be a Monkee in October. The voice I heard had something in mind for me.'

I had read articles that claimed that The Monkees couldn't play instruments and couldn't sing. I asked Peter to share the truth. He quickly responded: 'There were two rumors, one was we couldn't and one was we didn't. The one that we couldn't is not true; the one that we didn't was true. We were four actors hired to do a TV show. And in fact, as I look back, we could not have made records of the quality and the rate they needed. The whole operation had to be in full gear right away. And they had professional music makers and professional record makers that they knew they could count on,' Tork said.

However, as The Monkees' popularity skyrocketed, so did their interest in making and performing their own music. 'I believe that we ramped up eventually to the point that we could have been making our own records on an ongoing basis. In fact, our third album was *Headquarters* and we made that album ourselves,' Tork said, reflecting back.

'Now, looking back, I see the why and how. It makes all kinds of sense. If I were doing a parallel kind of an operation today, I'd do it exactly the same way,' stated Tork.

The Monkees would go on to sell more than 75 million records worldwide, making them one of the biggest selling groups of all time, with hits that include 'Daydream Believer', 'Pleasant Valley Sunday', 'Last Train to Clarksville' and 'I'm a Believer'. *The Monkees* TV series produced 58 episodes between September 1966 and March 1968. The series won two Emmy Awards in 1967.

It was a thrill and an opportunity to reminisce about The Monkees with one of its key members, Peter Tork. I found Peter to be funny, intelligent, candid and honest. Peter Tork passed away on February 21st, 2019 at home in eastern Connecticut at the age of 77. The cause of death was complications from a rare form of cancer that was first diagnosed in 2009.

Tim Conway – Actor and Comedian

Actor and comedian Tim Conway was a guest on *Profiles* in the spring of 2015. At the time of our interview he was passing through New York City on a promotional tour with the release of his memoir titled *What's So Funny*. I was thrilled to have Mr. Conway as a guest on the show. I had been a long time fan of his work, which included eleven years starring on *The Carol Burnett Show*, and as the bumbling Ensign Charles Parker in the TV sitcom *McHale's Navy* from 1962 through 1966. More recently, Conway made numerous guest appearances while winning Emmys for roles on such shows as *Coach* and *30 Rock*. In later years, he reunited with *McHale's Navy* sidekick Ernest Borgnine doing voiceover work in *SpongeBob Squarepants*.

As a kid, Conway suffered from dyslexia. 'Yes, especially in high school. When I had to get up and read aloud I used to live in fear of the days they would call on me. It got to be very humorous, so I thought I must be funny and why not go into comedy,' Conway remembered.

In his book, I read that he originally started out in radio. So I asked Tim whether radio offered a good foundation for what was to follow in his show business career. Laughing, Conway replied, 'I worked for a disc jockey in Cleveland, Big Wilson. He had a canary that he would play the piano for and the canary would sing. Most of my stuff I wrote for him ended up at the bottom of the birdcage.' While at the radio station Tim was offered to go out to the west coast to try out for a part in a new TV series *McHale's Navy*. He was reluctant. 'I really didn't want to go, I was happy at the radio station. The station manager told me if I stay here he'd fire me. So I decided to go west and give it a try,' Conway said.

Out of high school, Conway enlisted in the Army and laughably showed up a day early for duty. 'I got the dates mixed up. I eventually spent two years and two weeks in the Army. I got court-martialed, so they put the extra two weeks at the end. I was on guard duty one night guarding ping pong balls. I fell asleep in my car and left my rifle in the trunk. When I got back to my post I noticed a large neon light bulb in the garbage and used it as my rifle. Then a lieutenant came by and asked me what I was carrying. I told the lieutenant that it was a light bulb and that if he came any closer that I would turn it on. For that I got an extra two weeks in the Army,' Conway laughed.

Regarding his role as Ensign Parker in the hit series *McHale's Navy*, Conway said: 'He was an offbeat silly guy who thought he knew everything, and knew nothing.' In the 60s and 70s Tim starred on *The Carol Burnett Show*, which had 30 million people tuning in every week. 'It was Carol's show and she was one of the nicest, most generous people in show business. Carol is even better than the myth surrounding her,' Conway reflected. *The Carol Burnett Show* stayed at the top of the ratings for eleven years. 'We did a Broadway show once a week, with costumes and a twenty-six piece orchestra. That's why you don't see that kind of show anymore, it was so expensive to do,' Conway lamented.

In the late 60s, Tim starred in his own situation comedy western called *Rango*, which *TV Guide* ranked at number 47 among the 50 worst shows of all time. I asked Tim, 'What was it about *Rango* that earned it that kind of notoriety?' Nearly falling out of his chair laughing, Conway said, 'I don't think people liked making fun of westerns. It wasn't me, I was very humorous.'

I finished up by asking Mr. Conway, 'What might your fans be surprised to learn about you?' Tim quickly responded, 'I have an obligation to people, to help them and make them laugh. I feel very lucky that I'm in this business and have been somewhat of a success. Because of this, I'm always the first one to volunteer when there's a worthy benefit.'

Tim Conway passed away on May 21st, 2019 in Los Angeles, as a result of water in the brain. He was 85.

Rutger Hauer - Actor

Blond, blue-eyed, tall and handsome best describes this accomplished Dutch actor. Rutger had established a reputation for playing everything from romantic leads to action heroes to sinister villains. He had worked non-stop since 1973, and you may recognize him in films such as *Blind Fury*, *Blade Runner*, *The Hitcher*, *Sin City* and *Nighthawks*, just to mention a few. During our interview, we discussed his Dutch heritage, along with doing an unsuccessful stint in the Dutch Navy which was cut short when they discovered that he was colorblind, resulting in a medical release.

We also talked about his experience working opposite Sylvester Stallone in *Nighthawks*, which Rutger admitted didn't go all that well. According to Rutger: 'We were doing a stunt on the Roosevelt tram in New York City, Sylvester made a mistake with the cable and harness and nearly killed me... I was not a happy camper.' Although I thoroughly enjoyed my interview with Rutger, I couldn't help but notice how nervous he seemed. I watched him fidget in the chair across from me, seemingly uncomfortable throughout the entire interview. Then, it dawned upon me: Rutger was phenomenal at playing a multitude of characters in various films, but not so good at playing Rutger. He was not comfortable in his own skin. Every insecurity surfaced. As soon as the interview ended, Rutger leaned over to me, shoulders slumped as he sighed with relief, 'Boy, am I glad that's over with!'

Rutger Hauer passed away on July 19, 2019, at his home in the Netherlands from an undisclosed illness. He was 75.

Chapter 13
Keys To Effective Interviewing

I'm often asked, 'What are the keys to becoming an effective interviewer?' I've always felt that the question is a valid one. It's not one I think about often, but when I do, I realize that many things go into the process. So here's my attempt to answer that question: the six major keys to effective interviewing.

1. Research

Without a doubt, research is at the top of the list. Nothing is more unprofessional than going into an interview unprepared or even half prepared. When a guest senses the interviewer in unprepared they deem it as disrespectful. It's important to note that time is valuable, especially amongst celebrities. So most guests rightfully expect the interviewer to be fully prepared.

Once I schedule a guest for an interview, the research process begins. If they have a new book, I read it. If they have a new CD, I listen to it. If they have a new movie or television series, I read the reviews and attempt to learn as much as possible regarding the project. In preparation, I also like to research past interviews and articles, to learn as much as possible regarding the evolution of my guest. Nothing is more effective than pulling out quotes from previous interviews or articles to get the guest to open up about the topics you want to cover.

As an interviewer, you should always have an outline of the direction that you'd like the interview to go. If the interview requires some tough questions, I've always felt that it works best if you lead up to them, rather than starting out with them. In some cases, if you begin with the tough questions, the guest may feel pressured or even insulted. I've seen guests walk out of interviews if they feel the interviewer came on too strong or was disrespectful right from the start. As an interviewer, you have an obligation to ask the tough questions. Picking the right time to ask the tough questions is an art and a skill that an interviewer nurtures with time.

Always have more questions than the allotted time requires, especially on live television. For example, many years ago, I was hosting a show called *Staten Island Live* for Time Warner Cable. It was live television. One night I was interviewing a detective about the elimination of gang formation in the community. I was allotted fifteen minutes for the interview. The detective answered every question with quick, one sentence responses. Five minutes into the interview I was out of questions. All I can remember was peeking over at the director, who was frantically rolling his hands to keep going while holding up ten fingers. This meant that I had ten minutes on live television to go - and I was out of questions. Talk about a nightmare scenario; I was deep inside one! Somehow we chatted for another ten minutes, but to this day I can't remember what about. However, that night I learned an important lesson. If you have a fifteen-minute interview, prepare for a twenty-minute one. Always do more research that you need to and always have more questions than the actual time allotted might require.

Two of my past guests on *Profiles* were Dr. Maya Angelou and Deepak Chopra, both of whom I would consider to be intellectuals. To be honest, as I prepared for both interviews I wondered to myself if I wasn't in way over my head. I knew I was, but needed to prepare and figure out a way to pull both interviews off. The key to success that leveled the playing field for me was my diligent research and preparation. They both realized during the interviews that I had done my homework and reciprocated by making me feel like I belonged. I consider both interviews excellent and credit my research and preparation in the end result.

2. Pre-Interview

Sometimes guests like to conduct a brief pre-interview so they can become comfortable and prepared for the actual interview. I've always tried my best to avoid this process, mainly because I hate when the person I'm interviewing appears affected and rehearsed. So I've always tried my best to talk my guests out of a pre-interview.

However, what I do like to do is meet my guest prior to the interview. I like to talk to them about their hobbies and interests unrelated to the upcoming interview. I've found that this kind of conversation relaxes them and in some cases creates the beginning of a bond. If the pre-interview conversation goes well, when the camera starts rolling for real, the on-air atmosphere is usually much more relaxed right from the start.

If I must do a pre-interview, I try to be as brief and general as possible. I always keep the specific and tough questions for the actual interview.

I've always felt that some of my best interviews involved questions that surprised my guests. I can't tell you how many times a guest has said during the interview: 'Wow, that's great, where did you get that!?' However, the resulting answer is usually interesting and compelling. Always save those kinds of questions for when the cameras are rolling.

3. Appearance

How to dress for the interview? For the most part, I'm old school. I always wear a suit and tie, and always make sure my shoes are shined.

Over the years most of my guests have commented on how great and professional they felt I looked. For me, it's simply a form of respect for our guest and our show. I've always felt that if you want to be taken seriously as a journalist, you should dress like a professional.

From time to time, I've had news directors and even station managers suggest that I dress down a bit. I have continuously fought against this and will continue to do so. Always look your best, it will garner respect!

4. On-Air Persona

I've always felt that one of the keys to an effective interview is to appear relaxed on camera. I've never tried to be an interviewer, instead, I've always tried to be myself. My ultimate goal is that viewers will get the feeling that the interviews are taking place in my living room or theirs, not a sterile television studio.

My mentor, former New York City Fox anchor Bill McCreary, once told me: 'Never let them see you sweat!' It sounds simple, but it's not. It takes trial and error and experience.

There are two things that have always bothered me about other interviewers. First, those who are obviously trying to act like an interviewer instead of just being themselves. And second, interviewers who take themselves way too seriously. It's ok to make mistakes; God knows I've made a ton of them. It's also ok to laugh at yourself and incorporate some humor into the interview from time to time. It will make you appear human and likable in many cases! As the Joker said, 'Why so serious?' Loosen up, relax, and most importantly have fun and enjoy the experience. Not everyone can be Walter Cronkite. Find your on-air persona, fine tune it, study it, get feedback about it and go on to be the best you can be.

As an interviewer, I learned early on that you can't always control interviews. This includes tempo, content, and result. For example, when I had Broadway legend Ben Vereen as a guest on *Profiles*, I started the interview off by asking him a basic introductory question: 'Hi Ben, welcome to *Profiles*, it's an honor having you on the show; how have you been?' Ben was more than happy to answer that question and proceeded to go on for fifteen minutes with an array of stories and tales. However, a good interview requires a give and take environment, and Ben would not allow me to get back into the conversation to ask another question. Since the show is taped and not live, I had the ability to briefly stop the interview and ask Ben if he would be so kind as to shorten his responses. It was a thirty-minute program and I had many more questions that I would still like to ask. Ben apologized as I directed the producer to once again get the cameras rolling. I asked Ben my second question and just like the first Ben went off on another ten-minute storytelling spree.

In order to get the interview I wanted, we talked for a little over sixty minutes, half of which we edited out to produce our thirty-minute episode. This was a tough assignment even for the best of editors. Ben meant well, he's just an old school storyteller. Reflecting back, it was an interview that I had little control over. In the end, I kept my patience, which is the key lesson here, and did whatever I had to do to get another episode produced.

In another interview, I had Matt Roloff as a guest on the show. For more than a decade Matt's been starring on his television reality series *Little People, Big World* on the TLC Network. On the show, four foot tall Matt faces a variety of challenges in raising his four children on their 34-acre Oregon farm.

In doing my research, I read that Matt had been pulled over by police while driving home one day and was issued a DWI violation. During the interview I asked Matt about the DWI, and Matt responded: 'To be honest, I seldom drink. However, that day I did have a few beers in town and unfortunately got pulled over on the way home.' After Matt's explanation, I changed the subject and moved on to other questions.

A few hours later Matt called me from the airport as he was waiting to board his flight back to Oregon. 'Mickey, would it be possible to take the part about the DWI violation out of our interview?' Matt asked. He then explained: 'Little people have long been stereotyped as little drunks and I have worked extremely hard to overcome that stereotype along with many others. And as I mentioned, this was one isolated, unfortunate circumstance and mistake.'

After careful consideration, I decided to eliminate that part of the interview. I felt that Matt had made a horrible mistake but was extremely remorseful for it. He was also a really nice person who has dedicated his life to making things better for little people around the world. I didn't want to air anything that might derail his progress.

As an interviewer, these kinds of editorial decisions are a part of the job. They are decisions that I find myself having to make consistently.

5. Keep Learning

I've had the honor of interviewing actors Eli Wallach and Ernest Borgnine when they were both well into their 90s. Both candidly admitted that they work on their craft every day and always aspire to get better at what they do.

As I close in on my 500th episode of *Profiles*, I think I've watched every frame of every episode and more than once! Why? To get better! I don't think I've ever conducted an interview in which, after watching it, I didn't find things that could have been altered or improved upon. It could be as simple as the pronunciation of a word, the way I asked a specific question, or in some cases, the lack of a compelling follow-up question that I failed to ask.

TV personality Kandi Burruss once said during our *Profiles* interview: 'When you think you've made it, and convince yourself that you're on top, there's only one way to go but down.'

Create a work ethic that no matter how successful you become you continuously strive to improve. Always feel that your best work is yet ahead if you.

Don't be afraid to listen and take advice from others; sometimes their interest in what you're doing may help you improve, and in some cases, keep you on top.

I was lucky in the mentor department; I cut my teeth at Fox News in New York City. I got to watch and learn from polished professionals such as John Roland, Jim Ryan, Rosanna Scotto,

Maury Povich, Pablo Guzman and my mentor Bill McCreary. And I did so WAY before ever getting in front of a camera for real. Many interviewers, hosts, and reporters look in the wrong direction for feedback on their performance. Of course, Uncle Joe is going to tell you that you are great. Instead, find a seasoned professional to critique your work. Most will give you an honest assessment along with suggestions on how to improve and get better.

If you can't take criticism and don't have the desire nor the need to improve then you're probably in the wrong business.

Most interviewers have both strengths and weaknesses. Identify both, then improve on your strengths, and strive to overcome or eliminate your weaknesses.

<u>6. Stay Classy</u>

Over my twenty-five years within the broadcasting industry, I've interviewed some of the biggest stars in show business. I've also worked with and watched in action some of the best broadcast journalists in television. Each has left a lasting impression with me, some good, some not so good.

Frank Sinatra once said: 'If you're on time you're late.' As the coach of my production team, I always ask each member to allow ample time for set-up, usually at least one hour before the actual interview.

When preparing for a television interview, the crew led by Senior Producer and Editor of twenty years Monina Montenegro, is typically made up of one, two, and in some cases three camera operators. Also, our crew usually consists of a producer, lighting technicians, and a sound technician. I always refer to this crew as my team! And everyone on it plays an important role in the success of the interview.

Setting up cameras, obtaining the best lighting and sound is a skill set that develops with time and is a vital part of pulling off a professional interview. I always have a producer behind the camera that's on me. The producer's main job is to let me know, through hand signals, exactly where I am within the interviews, how much time is left, and when to close the interview.

The golden rule amongst the team members is: if something goes wrong with any of the equipment, stop the interview and troubleshoot the problem, fix it, and continue. Once a problem is identified, ignoring it might ruin the remainder of the interview. The only time all of this wouldn't apply would be for live television interviews. The rule here is to never stop, always keep going. Hopefully, technicians can work through the problem during the live taping.

A television crew is no different than a baseball or football team. Everyone has a role to play and should take pride in accomplishing their assigned task. With every interview I've conducted over the past twenty-five years, I can't ever remember one that had a perfect production. After watching our interviews, there's always something that could have been done better production-wise. Whether it be lighting, the position of a camera, or a prop on the set, always learn and strive to improve.

I often ask my entire crew to sit down as a group and watch a recent interview production. At the end, each offers their critique of the production. It has helped enormously towards consistent improvement and incorporated a desire among the team to be the best they can be. If everyone on the production crew feels equally important, success will surely follow.

I have always tried to lead by example, which includes treating everyone from the doorman to the most important person in the building with respect and compassion. In doing so, I always aspire for my team to follow suit.

Someone once told me, 'Better lucky than good.' However, when luck comes your way you better be prepared and ready for it, because it may be fleeting. Not everyone gets blessed with luck. Those who have been so blessed have, I've always felt, an obligation to be nice and cordial, especially to those less fortunate. How much effort does it take to shake a hand, sign an autograph, or take a picture with someone? I've always been surprised by those who grow reluctant to do so. In most cases the fans who support them are the reasons that successful celebrities are where they are today.

A few years ago Lady Gaga was making her new music video 'Marry The Night' literally right outside of my office on Staten Island. It was a million dollar production and I got to witness the process first hand. Most of the shooting occurred at night, and yes, there was tight security. However, seven or eight of her fans known as Little Monsters worked their way onto the set. When Lady Gaga realized that her seven or eight Little Monsters had been standing outside most of this chilly evening, Gaga ordered pizza for the group. What a thoughtful gesture from one of the music industry's biggest stars. Lady Gaga won me over that night, and it's easy to see why she is so loved and successful.

Never forget where you come from and always cherish those who support you, and most importantly, always STAY CLASSY!

Final Thoughts on Being Effective

Stay Away From Negativity

My mother would often say to me: 'Misery loves company.' That's especially true with negative people. Don't allow negativity into your world; always search for the positivity in everything you do. Surround yourself with positive people and they will lift you towards success. One of my mother's favorite quotes was: 'When the character of a man is not clear to you, look at his friends.' Seek out friends who enhance your goals and dreams and as my father often reminded me: 'Tell me who your friends are and I'll tell you who you are.' Susan Lucci said during our *Profiles* interview: 'It takes a village to be successful.' My advice to anyone is to fill your village with positive people.

Stay Driven

Singer and television personality Kandi Burruss said during our interview: 'Getting to the top is really hard. Staying there is even harder. When you convince yourself that you've made it, you're most likely setting yourself up for a fall.'

Fight against complacency and always keep sight of the next goal you're looking to accomplish. Kandi is a great example: she's found success as a singer, songwriter, a record producer, television personality, actress and entrepreneur. 'I work hard every day to stay focused and driven with all facets of my career,' Burruss said.

Another reason to stay driven comes from former professional baseball great Satchel Paige when he said: 'Don't look back. Something or someone might be gaining on you.'

Step Out of Your Comfort Zone

Challenge yourself; don't be afraid to try new things that could possibly enhance your life and career. For example, when I was in high school the thought of public speaking would give me panic attacks. I would do everything within my power to avoid public speaking situations. Even in my classes, when I was asked to get up and speak or read something, I would make up some dumb excuse to get out of it, such as I don't feel well or I forgot my glasses, etc. I later learned that the fear of public speaking was the number one fear in our society.

Determined to overcome my fear, some years later while attending Missouri Valley College I enrolled in every speaking class that was available. They included Public Speaking I and II, Advanced Public Speaking and Speech and Drama. Little by little I conquered my fear. Since then, I've spoken in public hundreds of times; I even gave the keynote address to thousands in attendance for the graduation ceremony at my Alma Mater Missouri Valley College in 2012.

If I had not stepped out of my comfort zone to battle and overcome my fear of public speaking I would never have been equipped to pursue my dream of attaining a broadcasting career as I have.

Repetition

According to Webster's Dictionary, repetition is defined as a thing repeated. I have always been a strong believer in repetition: the more you do the same thing, the better you will get at that task.

My high school football coach Sal Somma broke the mold on incorporating repetition into his coaching and teaching philosophy. We would practice the same plays over and over again. I didn't appreciate it back then, but eventually, I got it. The key to producing in sports is to be able to perform at peak efficiency under pressure. When the game is on the line, can you pull off the big play that can catapult you to victory? Why do some players on teams always seem to come up with the big play when it's most needed? My high school football team was one that consistently produced that big play when it was most needed; the reason, repetition in practice. We could run those plays in our sleep. So when we had to execute at a critical time in the game, we were able to so because we had consistently repeated the task multiple times before.

When I coached high school basketball some years later, I incorporated Coach Somma's philosophy regarding repetition into my practice routine. My teams ran their offense beautifully, and I credit repetition as the key in being able to accomplish this, especially under pressure. We won many close games over my tenure as a head coach. I attributed all those wins to the repetition philosophy in practice every day and the discipline that comes along as a by-product of repetition.

When I had former NFL great Joe Montana as a guest on *Profiles* we discussed his teammate Jerry Rice, who is considered to be among the best wide receivers in NFL history. According to Montana: 'Jerry practiced every day at full speed; everything he did was all out. He repeated the same moves over and over again. I credit his practice philosophy for much of his success." At the end of his career, Mr. Rice ranked first among NFL All-Purpose yards gained of All-Time, with 25,546 yards.

I feel the same holds true as a philosophy in the broadcasting industry. Repeat the things you need to be good at until they become second nature. Repeating specific tasks will allow you to be the best you can be when you need it the most… especially under pressure.

Set Short and Long Term Goals

Setting goals is vital! Many people make the mistake of establishing one major goal. For example, their goal is to be an anchor at NBC in New York City. My suggestion would be to also create some smaller goals while always striving to achieve the major one. For example, when I decided to pursue a career in broadcasting, my first goal was to get my foot in the door within the industry.

I did so by getting a job as a sound man on the news crews at Fox in New York City. My ultimate goal was to someday host an interview show like I do today. I accomplished my ultimate goal by achieving smaller ones along the way. I went from sound man to field producer, to reporter and finally to host. Achieving the little goals along the way gave me the confidence, knowledge, and experience necessary to achieve the big ones. Achieving the little goals will always help from getting discouraged during one's journey.

Persevere

Don't ever let others tell you that you can't do something. Believe in your dream and never give up on it. When I was interviewing professional boxer George Foreman on *Profiles*, he said: 'When I decided to make a comeback in my forties everyone told me that I was too old.' George started his comeback at the bottom, fighting lesser known fighters. On November 5th, 1994, he once again became a heavyweight champion at age 45, knocking out Michael Moorer. George broke three records that night. At age 45 he became the oldest fighter to win the World Heavyweight Championship; 20 years after losing his title for the first time, he broke the record for the fighter with the longest interval between his first and second world championship; and the age spread of 19 years between champion and challenger was the largest of any heavyweight boxing championship fight.

As George said during our interview: 'Don't let anyone tell you that you can't do something.'

Instant Gratification

If there's something I've learned throughout my life it's that there is no such thing as instant gratification. Everything takes time, and as my mother often reminded me, patience is a virtue. It takes years to become an effective actor, singer, athlete and in my case broadcaster. During my interview with Federico Castelluccio, who played Furio Giunta on the HBO hit series *The Sopranos*, he remarked: 'It usually takes about ten years to make it as an actor in New York City.' He went on to say: 'Those who stick with it eventually find their niche within the industry.'

It's been my experience that those who seek instant gratification, regardless of the profession, usually don't last, and drop out way before the race is finished.

Joan Rivers said during our *Profiles* interview: 'Most of the comedians I started out with, who stuck with it, eventually became successful within some facet of the comedy world.' The key phrase is 'Stuck with it.' Don't expect instant gratification; anything worth working and fighting for will take time, trial and error and most importantly excessive amounts of determination and hard work.

Be Nice to Everyone

Some believe that kindness is a weakness; however, I feel that it's actually a strength. Being kind is always honorable, and in many instances, the best way to fight your battles is with kindness.

During a *Profiles* interview with Deepak Chopra, he said: 'The best way to fight your enemy is with love, then they will be your friend.'

Being mean doesn't solve anything other than to create enemies. In my interview with actor Eric Roberts, we discussed that early in his career he had a serious problem with cocaine. The result of his drug use was that he would become nasty with everyone involved in the films he was working on. Cocaine made him belligerent and almost impossible to get along with. This behavior hindered his career and kept him in smaller parts instead of the Hollywood leading man roles that he should have starred in. Reflecting back Eric said: 'When you're not nice to people - and in my case, I was really awful to many - sooner or later most of those people will rise up out of the ashes to get even, and they did.'

Personally, after nearly 500 *Profiles* episodes I can honestly say that those guests who treated me and my crew with kindness are the ones who have a special place in my heart. Their kindness made everything better for me and my crew and we will never forget the gesture. It all comes down to the Golden Rule: Do unto others as you would have them do unto you. Try it, it really works.

Be Creative

Creativity is a skill you can work on with time, training and effort. Consistently broaden your knowledge by reading, writing and listening to music; all will sharpen your creativity. We recently had singer and actress Melba Moore on *Profiles*. Melba has long been recognized for her soaring four-octave range. In 1970 she won a Tony Award for Best Performance by a Featured Actress in a Musical on Broadway for her role in *Purlie*. Today, at 74 years old, Melba is still at the top of her game and continues to perform all over the world, but understands that she has to be disciplined and creative to stay there. 'I treat my voice like an athlete treats their bodies. My voice is a gift from God, but I have to be extremely vigilant to give it the nutrition, exercise and rest that it requires. My voice is actually stronger today than it's ever been,' Melba said.

Aspire to be an expert in a specific area. Researchers estimate that being world class or the best at anything requires a minimum of 10,000 hours of practice. Jeanette 'The Black Widow' Lee, who rose to become the number one professional pool player in the world, said during her interview on *Profiles*, 'I would practice 48 hours straight until I became so exhausted that my friends would have to carry me home.' Create a practice routine that involves pushing yourself to master tasks that go beyond your perceived capabilities.

Get a mentor. Learn from your mentor. However, don't try to be like your mentor. Create your own style that is one hundred percent you. Be different from the pack; your individuality will make you stand out and get noticed. Of my nearly five hundred episodes of *Profiles*, each guest had something unique about them that made them stand out; they had an X-factor that made them special. Find your X-factor, groom it, and make it work for you.

Learn and understand what environment allows you to be the most creative. For example, Smokey Robinson, who's written over four hundred songs, said during our *Profiles* interview: 'I got some of my best ideas for writing songs while cruising in my car.' For others, they may feel most creative in the office, at home, sitting on the beach, or even just taking a walk. Identify what environment works best for you and utilize it for your creative periods.

'All work and no play makes Jack a dull boy' may not be an ancient Chinese proverb, but it is wisdom nonetheless. It basically means that without time off from work, a person becomes both bored and boring. Too much work can also lead to becoming uninspired, or burnt out. For me, I love playing golf to de-stress. I've found it to be a great outlet to clear my head and refresh my creativity. The key is, you have to make time for your outlet, no matter what that outlet may be. Many people I talk to regarding outlets say things such as 'I don't have the time', or 'I'm too busy with work and family' etc. I always respond by saying, 'Think of your outlet as creative medicine.' Making time for a round of golf isn't always easy for me, but I understand the mental advantages that it affords me. In the days following a round of golf with friends, I usually feel more energized, happier and more creative.

Many researchers feel that creativity is a learned behavior, and that non-creative behavior is also learned. My conclusion is that creativity is a muscle that can be developed with consistent exercise, practice and positive habits. It's really as simple as 'Use it or lose it'.

Tips and Tricks

If there's one thing I've learned over my twenty-five years in front of the camera, it's how to dress, and how not to dress. For example, avoid loud ties with small patterns, they have a tendency to dance on camera. The same is true for suits; try to stick with solid colors. As for shirts, don't wear white, because the bright lights will wash you out and make you look overexposed. I suggest light blue, light green or beige dress shirts.

Body language is very important. Sit erect but not ramrod-straight. I try to visualize that I'm interviewing guests in my living room. I always aspire to create a relaxed environment. Avoid signs of discomfort or anxiety such as foot tapping, shifting back and forth, moving your head all over the place and fist clenching. These nervous habits make the interviewer appear like an amateur, and make the guests uncomfortable. You should also avoid sudden body movements. They will be distracting to the guest and will make it difficult for the videographer to keep you framed properly. Fighting nervousness is a skill set that improves with time. I've always felt that arriving early has helped me immensely. Getting accustomed to the surroundings early always gave me the feeling that the guest was entering my domain, which relaxed me. It also gave me ample time to review my notes and to visualize how I would like the interview to go. Arriving early also gives the technicians the opportunity to do their jobs more effectively, such as getting the sound levels and lighting exactly right. And if they do run into a technical issue, arriving early will give them the time to troubleshoot any problems that may occur.

If makeup is available, use it. High definition cameras will pick up most facial imperfections. I use a pancake makeup that I apply with a small sponge usually five or ten minutes prior to interviews. With the hot lights on most sets, applying makeup will conceal any sweating to some degree.

And lastly, many interviewers make the mistake of talking about themselves and interjecting their own personal experiences into interviews. For example, if the guest is discussing his collaboration with Smokey Robinson on a new album, no one wants to hear that the interviewer once met Smokey at a New York Jets football game. Always keep your focus and questions aimed entirely on the guest, that's why people are tuning in, because they want to learn more about the guest being interviewed. Most couldn't care less about the trials and tribulations of the interviewer.

Chapter 14
The Legacy Question

According to Webster, a legacy is defined as anything handed down from the past. In my almost 500 episodes of *Profiles*, I was always interested in what these accomplished people wanted to hand down to the next generation. And just as importantly, how did they hope to be best remembered? So I decided to end each and every episode with the question: 'What do you hope that your legacy will be?' It turned out to be the perfect question. A profile is defined as a concise overview; the legacy question was like a ribbon on a gift or the icing on the cake. It fit like a glove.

And so, I've also decided to end this book just like every television episode of *Profiles*, in sharing a cross section of responses to the legacy question.

What do you hope your legacy will be?

"I want to be the last man on earth without a cell phone"
-Jesse Ventura, Actor, Wrestler, Politician

"I would like my tombstone to read gonged at last"
-Chuck Barris, TV Show Creator

"She slept with them all"
-Joan Rivers, Comedian

"That I was a good person, that I lived a good life, that I was the best I could be"
-Rita Coolidge, Singer, Songwriter

"Hopefully that I was a good entertainer, period"
-Tony Orlando, Entertainer

"I hope my daughters love me"
-Robert Wagner, Actor

"I would love to get into the Hall of Fame, who wouldn't?"
-Keith Hernandez, Professional Baseball Player

"That I've inspired people to do better"
-Tamera Mowry, Actress

"There is a whole generation of kids that started watching our show when they were ten years old and now they're graduating college. I think in the future I'll look back and say, there's a whole generation of children that this is the show they grew up with"
-James Murray, Impractical Jokers Star

"Sitting down with Mickey to talk about my life, I mean that kind of thing is very, very important"
-Judy Collins, Singer

"Just that here's a guy with a partner made a lot of people happy"
-Bill Medley, Singer

"Teaching the next generation something that I can hand off to them, and then they can carry it on to the seventh generation. Additionally, running the company safely with a brand that's associated with quality"
-Phil Grucci, CEO Fireworks By Grucci

"Keep movin'... Jump to the next rock"
-Lee Grant, Actress

"I think that I was a good dad and a good husband. Second of all, that I was a good American and that I tried my best to influence more in their country"
-Lee Greenwood, Singer, Songwriter

"The lives that I touched, the people that I've helped, that's what I want my legacy to be"
-Darryl 'DMC' Daniels, Run-DMC, Rock 'N' Roll Hall of Fame

"That he wrote catchy songs, and that he was sincere when he sang. Finally, that he was also a neat guy"
-Stephen Bishop, Singer, Songwriter

"I hope that people think that I was a great musician"
-Kenny G, Musician

"Now I don't care about my legacy professionally. I care about it as a person, that I helped other people"
-Lisa Lampanelli, Comedian

"Just hope I was entertaining"
-Bruce Campbell, Actor

"That I was a sincere student of music"
-Eddie Palmeri, Musician

"I hope that I'm looked at as an artist that made people feel their deepest emotions"
-Mindi Abair, Musician & Saxophone Player

"I hope that I'm able to pass down some amazing things for my children and that I was able to do a lot of great things for women"
-Kandi Burruss, Actress, Singer

"I want to be remembered as a nice guy. A guy you can say hi to, a guy you don't feel embarrassed to come up to get an autograph or take a picture with"
-Bobby Rydell, Singer

"People overrate legacy. I would like to say that I should be forgotten as soon as somebody takes what I have done to the next level"
-Deepak Chopra, Author, Holistic & Alternative Advocate, Public Speaker

"I think I will always be remembered for Erika Kane"
-Susan Lucci, Actress

"I would like to be remembered as an artist who opened people up. To open up and heal or their minds to open up and have a different perspective on life"
-Gloria Reuben, Actress

"I hope my legacy is that I'm trying to be a decent human being. It's quite simple for me"
-Graham Nash, Singer

"She wasn't afraid to speak the truth if it would help others"
-Mackenzie Phillips, Actress

"I hope to break even"
-Gino Vannelli, Singer

"I'd like to be remembered as the queen of metal"
-Lita Ford, Guitarist

"My tombstone is going to read... I told you I was sick"
-Meatloaf, Singer

"She made us laugh"
-Vicki Lawrence, Actress

"I'm a huge believer in teaching an old dog new tricks. I'm always looking to try something new"
-Gretchen Carlson, Broadcast Journalist

"What have I contributed? Has my life been worthwhile? Most importantly, that I'm remembered as a nice person and a good person"
-Dawn Wells, Actress

"Gary Grant once told me, Rich do you realize what you do on stage... you bring people joy and happiness for about an hour and a half. You take them out of their humdrum life and make them feel good about themselves... that's a gift! I hope that's what my Legacy will be"
-Rich Little, Impressionist

"I hope I would have brought some joy to some people. I do come across some people who say you helped us through some really bad times. That brings me enormous pleasure, and what we're inclined to do as performers... We make a record and we walk away from it, but of course, going out there and touching people and we're inclined to forget that. That's what I would like to think that I would be remembered for, bringing some joy to people"
- **Petula Clark**, Singer, Songwriter

"My legacy is what I hear today. When I turn on the radio, I hear people singing who've been gone for a while and are still ever present because they put down those magic moments on music and lyrics and that's how I'd like to be remembered"
-Engelbert Humperdinck, Singer

"That he didn't take no shit from no one. You'll have to bleep that. I want my legacy to be that Jesse Ventura was a free thinker, who never worried about questioning authority"
-Jesse Ventura, Actor, Wrestler, Politician

"Basically, that Sheila was a good, inspiring person. Everyone knows that I love what I do and the passion behind it and I'll do it until I can't do it anymore and hopefully I made a difference in the world"
-Sheila E, Percussionist

"Versatility, my initial goal when I started out, even though my mom and dad didn't want me to venture down a path that is strewn with all kinds of problems and obstacles. I wanted to be a pop artist and a classical artist all at the same time. People said you can be one or the other but you can't be both"
-Stacy Keach, Actor

"I hear from people that my music helped them get through teenage years, suicide attempts, army stints, jail terms, helped serenade people down a wedding aisle, helped serenade people into making a baby. I hope people were pleased by my time here"
-Melissa Manchester, Singer, Songwriter

"That I was honest in what I was doing, and that I loved what I was doing"
-Danny Aiello, Actor

"I don't think that a person deserves to be remembered for any more or any less than what they were. Different people will view you in different ways... How I would like to be remembered would be as someone trying to treat people good"
-Charlie Daniels, Band Leader, Singer, Songwriter

"I hope that people are inspired by the courage that I had or the roles that I have been gratefully able to play and that I've impacted their lives in a positive way somehow"
-Chrissy Metz, Actress

"I just want to be known for my integrity and my purity, not morally, but as presenting the music in the best way I can"
-Jack Jones, Singer

"I really don't know. It's funny how people ask me about this bizarre Austin Powers connection which I have nothing to do with... I'd like to leave some records that people still enjoy to listen to but I don't look backward much but I look forward, I find myself very lucky that I'm 72 I have the same enthusiasm from making records and thank God there's so much going on that I don't have time to think in legacy terms"
-Peter Asher, Singer, Talent Management

"I hope that young people will learn to value words and not use words stupidly, think about what you're saying. Get rid of excess verbiage in your lyric writing. Sing melodies and sing notes and hit the notes because a lot of that is gone now"
-Don Mclean, Singer, Songwriter

"That I could hopefully get that variety show and do a little bit more for the whole industry and the people and the Lord will let me still sing till I'm the same age as George Burns, that I don't get Alzheimer's or none of that type of stuff and I can remember all that kinds of stuff"
-Charley Pride, Singer

"That it wasn't just about me. I did something that helped other people to change their lives. And that my art, years from now, people can go back and rediscover who I was

what I was trying to project, it tears me up saying it, and take something from that and be better than me"
-Malina Moye, Singer, Guitarist

"I think that the most important legacy right now is my family. I was very fortunate; I got one of these National Father of the Year awards for a number of years. I said at the luncheon that you can't be a Father of the Year without being married to the Wife and Mother of Every Year, 46 years my wife Dorothy has been fabulous. Not just about putting me through law school but everything else; we have two kids, our daughter is a cancer surgeon. You know I tell people I talk for a living, she saves people's lives. Our son is a banker, they both have wonderful spouses so for me when people say what are you most proud of I say take a look at my children, take a look at my family"
"Professionally people would say to me, I saw you reporting and I had no idea what you think about it and I say 'Great!' Someone once said to me, I learned from you on television when you would explain things to me, I didn't know how you felt about it but I understood it. And for me, if that's the legacy of my journalism, that I helped people understand it, I'd be delighted"
-Jack Ford, TV Legal Expert, Attorney

"She's a good kid"
-Julie Budd, Singer

"I don't know. I hope this book will still be available to people so they can read it, that would be pretty cool"
-Michael Imperioli, Actor, Author

"He could tell a story. He was equal to the moment when it required something like that. And that he was not a narcissist"
-Verne Lundquist, Sportscaster

"Well, my best years are ahead of me, the way I look at it. I have a 30-year-old guy in here *taps chest* but I got a 70-year-old body. He loves life, he loves to laugh, he likes to have fun"
- Little Anthony, Singer

"No one's ever asked me that before! I would like to think that I have left a lot of love behind"
-Helen Reddy, Singer

"I guess I would like to be well thought of by my fellow actors, actors of the actors equity association, members of the screen actors guild because the people who service those organizations work on them without any money, who do the contracts and negotiating, are the best people in the profession and most of them are not stars and not names that anybody knows but the time that they put into it benefits generations of actors after them, who have health insurance, who have minimum wage law, all kinds of benefits these people spent hours of their lives bringing about. I would say that is what I'm proudest of and that's something worth aspiring to"
-Tony Roberts, Actor

"Hard to say, if someone could say they saw you in concert and they remember it, that's a good feeling. If someone likes the music and goes into the sort of songbook, when 'Goody Two Shoes' is used for the Shrek soundtrack I'm gratified because it's another generation, my daughters are going to see it, younger kids will see it and that's good"
-Adam Ant, Singer

"I hope my legacy will be that I entertained a lot of people, made people happy, gave a lot of people hope and dreams that they can be like me, because I wasn't handed this key to success. I had to work very hard for it. I want people to look

185

at me and say 'If Sam can do it I can do it', being a working-class girl"
- **Samantha Fox,** Singer

"That's a good question. I would certainly know that I'm a mild personality. Like Charlie Pride told me when I left his show and I said, 'Thanks a lot for helping me Charlie' and he said, 'Pass it on.' I always want to do that, to help other people and to know anything because the records are so permanent"
-**Ronnie Milsap,** Singer

"I just want people to enjoy a night out. When I got into this business I said I'd be happy working as a comedian just making people laugh every night whether it be 15 minutes or an hour. If I can go up there and make you forget about your problems, if it's fun for you it's double fun for me. There's nothing better than making a group of people laugh. I'm not out here to change the world, to be political. I'm here to make people laugh with things they can relate to and that's it"
-**Sebastian Maniscalco,** Comedian

"That I made a positive impact on life itself. That I've done something that can be a positive example for people and I'm not just talking young people, I'm talking people period"
-**Smokey Robinson,** Singer, Songwriter

"I hope people look at my career as motivation for them. I didn't have an uncle in the business or a mom as a casting director. In Hollywood, there are a lot of family ties and it's very political. I hope that people remember that I'm proud of Hercules, I'm proud of Andromeda. I think I have many more things in me and I have movies coming out. I hope that I leave a legacy of sorts that people will say he did a good job and he's a good guy"
-**Kevin Sorbo,** Actor

"Just that I did my best. That I made use of what I have. I'm no Pavarotti and I'm not Sinatra but I've got some of the elements of both of them"
-Tom Wopat, Actor, Singer

"I just want to keep having fun. When I press on I want people crying. I'm a Leo so I love the drama of it. After that's done I want them laughing every time they say my name because remember just how great, fun exhilarating marvelous caring times we had together"
-Patti Austin, Singer

"I like to consider myself a soul singer not because I only play soul music but no matter what music I do I put my soul into it, and I want it to reach people in that place, where their soul is. I feel if that can be my legacy then I will be very very happy"
-Joan Osborne, Singer

"What I've done is I'm a guitar player that's been lucky and been able to create something that inspires other people. That's very nice, that would be my place, that I've inspired a certain number of bands today"
-Tony Iommi, Guitarist

"That he put out beautiful music like an artist on canvas. So that it could be there forever and ever so that it could be heard for years and years to come. Like wow, I can listen to Sam Cooke and he's no longer here but he's in my heart"
-Aaron Neville, Singer

"You know what, I have children now and I want to see them grow into these fantastic adults that I really want to be around and share. There's such a thing as feeling like this matriarchy but you want to be able to share it. There's nothing finer than sharing it. I was performing at Epcot to see my family out there, the whole front row was my family.

I swear to you I was grinning ear to ear. Sharing what you have to the most amount of people is the biggest gift, the greatest joy. Your legacy is something to share, and lives on. Lives within, inside the heart and lives on and that you the artist are able to share and feel. Being able to take it in is the greatest gift for oneself and the other people getting the joy receiving it. It's a real full circle, it has to be otherwise you didn't know what you did it all for"
-Taylor Dayne, Singer

"I would just like to be remembered as a person who made a difference in the world. Who went out and spoke out and who changed people's lives just by telling them to start over from their lives. By showing them there is a new path you can take. It's never too late to start over. No matter what it is, it doesn't have to be abuse, whatever your problems are you can always start over. And that's what is so important, we don't realize that we can always start over. I always say today is the first day of the rest of my life, make the most of it"
-La Toya Jackson, Singer, Author

"I don't think about my legacy. If they did write something on my tombstone, it'd just say Writer. And under that, 'The best!' No! The best Pete Hamill"
-Pete Hamill, Author

"What it is currently is when I walk down the street and people spot me they smile, that's my legacy. They don't say there goes that asshole. They say hey there goes Munch! It's nice to have a positive impact on people in general"
-Richard Belzer, Actor

"I would really like people to remember how much I really like working for them, the people, my fans because that's what I enjoyed doing and that's what I want people to remember"
-Darlene Love, Singer, Songwriter

"Someone who was a positive influence and not just in the sport of figure skating, in philanthropy, in life outside of the sport as well"
-Kristi Yamaguchi, 1992 Olympic Figure Skating Champion

"I think my legacy is defined, a guy of cool and style. I think this book is a revelation bringing back when I was a younger person and how creative I was. And now I'm out of the game and in broadcasting whatever I seem to touch I bring a measure of style and creativity to it and I believe that will be my legacy, one of the greatest Knicks ever. I think also willing to give back and always being cognizant of being a role model for our youth. If you ever come to The Garden there's always one autograph you're guaranteed you can get, take a picture. I feel humbled and honored that people hold me to such high esteem and I haven't played in multiple years. A new generation of kids now know me as the Knicks announcer. I'd be an ingrate to not be honored by my fans and to cater to their needs, sign an autograph, take a picture, making them happy at the games"
-Walt "Clyde" Frazier, Professional Basketball Player

"Right now there doesn't seem to be anything, when I look at it on a broad scale I don't see anything, what have I accomplished? Who knows about it? Big deal. Generations don't know about Chubby Checker, so what? To me, it's no big deal until it becomes a big deal. If I'm too old, if I get too old to participate in the rediscovery of Chubby Checker

they'll be celebrating by themselves. Because guess what I'm going to do, I'll say, too old now, thank you"
-Chubby Checker, Singer

"Truthfully, without sitting down here and trying to make something up really fast, I don't know. I'd like to think that in a couple of years I'll know what I'll have carved there on my tombstone. Still a work in progress, he died with his boots on or something like that"
-Duane "Dog" Chapman, Bounty Hunter

"My legacy would probably be, somebody that made it on his own and reached down and tried to pull up everybody that wanted to make it as well"
-Daymond John, Entrepreneur, one of the Sharks on the TV Show *Shark Tank*

"I'm still working 40 concerts a year. I'm hoping that people will still be humming the songs. I have a musical coming out in England March the First. It's called Laughter in the Rain, it's a story of my life from ages 15 to 35 and it's been quite a ride"
-Neil Sedaka, Singer, Songwriter

"I would hope that girls at home that look kinda like me and think kinda like me know that they have a place in show business and that they can make a living off of it now that someone has gone through the door"
-Tia Carrere, Actress

"I really hope as a musician we just don't play for ourselves and to certain people. I think we should do more things for the community. I hope music can help poor kids through different organizations. I really hope this foundation can help build music programs in public schools. And I really hope every kid can have a proper education in music"
-Lang Lang, Pianist

"Just that I liked to make people laugh. I never went into it to be 'a comedian'. When you see these folks after the show and they say it's the best show they've ever seen it's not just adulation, it's from their heart that they really had a good time, that people have a nice memory of that, of entertaining them live and people laughing and really enjoying themselves and taking them out of the grind of everyday life"
-Joe Piscopo, Comedian

"I hope that I will do my absolute very best in raising our children, it's a great responsibility, such an honor, and serving our customers. To be of service, that's what I want to do"
-Kathy Ireland, Supermodel, Entrepreneur

"That I was here, made a difference, helped people, very simple"
-Earl 'The Pearl' Monroe, Professional Basketball Player

"If I were saying it myself, she maintained her authenticity and individualism. I think that is most important. It's not really about if she was the greatest singer or she had the best style. It's the longevity in the context of the longevity the quality you did and the people along the way, you touched the people in some way with what you are doing as your passion"
-Jody Watley, Singer, Songwriter

"If you would have asked me that five years ago I would have said I hope I'm an academy winning actress, I've done 65 films and that's what I love to do. I say Man proposes and God disposes. I would like my legacy to be that of a healer. It's a very difficult world today. I just see so many people in pain. I've lost so many people in life. If someone would have taught me earlier. If I could just use my celebrity life at Playboy to save one life it would be worth it"
-Carol Alt, Supermodel, Author

"It's been wonderful over the years, and continuing to do so, to feel like I have entertained people, to have changed some people, touched their lives in a way. Maybe made them think and made them feel and enriched them in a way. That's the legacy of my work. As we spoke before some of the work is standing the test of time and I hope to make many more of those. I think my biggest legacy are my children and what they will do for this world, I'm always amazed by their beauty and their heart and their ability to make people smile. They have more charisma than me. They make people happy wherever they go. I hope to lead a life that is an example to them and one that will allow them to take off to wherever they go"
-Lou Diamond Phillips, Actor

"I'm hoping that I will enter the sci-fi hall of fame!"
-Ming Na, Actress

"That I'd be a compassionate human being and a really good actress"
-Marsha Mason, Actress

"Legacy? I don't expect to have a legacy. Oh, no. I think we all add something to this monument that American filmmaking is. If I brought a little that's good. I think acting has gone beyond with the technical development of lighting and sound and of film itself and all the techniques. I believe films have gotten better and better. All great films that have political content, emotional human content, I think they're fabulous. I think essential for the wellbeing of the population. They really fill you with joy when they're lovely"
-Leslie Caron, Actress

"Oh my God I have no ideas, I just want to go on. I'm more ambitious than ever in my life. The ambition hasn't died. You don't retire. You know what happens when you retire?

You die. Maybe it's because I haven't done everything I should have done or feel maybe I should have done it that way or maybe I have one more chance"
-Christopher Plummer, Actor

"That made stuff that made people feel, stuff that made people think. Stuff that makes people feel like they're not alone and other people are going through the same thing and thinking the same things, hopefully, a legacy of contribution that I contributed to this space we call ours, made it better and brought it to the next level"
-Tatyana Ali, Actress

"I hope, first and foremost they say Mario was a good guy, a nice guy, a genuine person, a gentleman. Did solid work, represented the community well, and represented the Latinos well. There's not too many people that look like me on television. Not too many Hispanics which is sort of sad given the demographic we represent. Hopefully, I'll do something about that and contribute to it later on." "You're somewhat of a pioneer for opening the floodgates for more Latinos to follow." "Well hopefully, I'm first generation, I'm from a border town, not so upscale town. So if a kid like me can do alright why can't anyone else"
-Mario Lopez, Television Host

"When it's all said and done that my children, grandchildren, and fans to remember that all the things that they're afraid to try and to explore and to record to go into it very passionately because all the aspects I've been involved with I loved"
-John Secada, Singer

"I want my legacy to be that I was a strong man, nothing to do with football. Strong, giving, a good man. That's what I tell people I want my little boy to be a stand-up and honest man"
-Herschel Walker, Professional Football Player

"Oh, I don't even care. Honestly, I really don't. I just do it to have fun, I do it to make a living. I think people get so into 'who are you, who are you known as'. I have reporters asking me what your next goal is. I don't know, I'm trying to do the best I can right now. George Carlin, one of the greatest comedians of all time, has evolved in three or four different stages in terms of what kind of comedy he did, do you think he thought about the next thing? I'm happy doing what I'm doing now. People will say you're not funny when you're not doing the impressions, you can't do this you can't do that. I don't care, it doesn't matter to me. I guess there is one little piece that sometimes the jokes aren't the impression but the comment after. That's the key. I just want to make the people laugh. People aren't going to learn a lot from me. I'm not a stand-up philosopher, some comedians make you come out of the theater saying Wow! I just want them to say, that made my life a little bit better, and that's what I hear after the show"
-Frank Caliendo, Comedian

"That my music is honest, that people recognize that with each and every adventure I gave my all, I gave my best"
-Gloria Gaynor, Singer

"I don't think much about this. George Bush does, Clinton does. I think that people that have legacies like Peter Schultz, creator of Peanuts, and Willie Nelson, come about accidentally. This is the difference between people like Governor Rick Perry and George Dubya who are elected who are important but admittedly not significant. They

194

managed to be important but not significant. Now Molly Ivins is significant, Mark Twain, of course, I was at his house about a week ago giving a speech. That's a significant man, you can't set out and say I'm going to be significant, you just have to do the very best you can. Be as honest as you can"
-Kinky Friedman, Musician

"I tell you what, who wouldn't want two tickets to paradise? Who doesn't want to take someone home tonight, who doesn't think they're in love and who doesn't want to go back? I wrote very tongue in cheek songs. My songs apply to everyday situations in life. When you're talking about two tickets to paradise you could be talking about taking a plane to Hawaii or maybe you're talking about putting a little extra money together to put enough gas in the car to drive up to the redwood country. People say what about the Rock 'n' Roll Hall of Fame? I'll tell you what, I'm from Long Island and being in the Long Island Rock 'n' Roll Hall of Fame is good enough for me. I'm sharing it with Neil Diamond, Blue Oyster Cult, KISS, a lot of great people. I'd love to get into the Rock 'n Roll Hall of Fame for my kids, my dad is in the Rock 'n' Roll Hall of Fame. Of course, you know it's very crowded, so many great musicians trying to get into the Rock 'n' Roll Hall of Fame. They're probably going to let me in when I'm an urn on my wife's fireplace. There's still a lot of time for them to let me in"
-Eddie Money, Singer

"Such a big question. I think I want to be remembered as 'oh he can play that, oh yeah he can play that too' 'he was a good actor but he can play 'A' really well and 'Z' too, he plays a great 'Z'"
-Eric Roberts, Actor

"I have a different hope for my legacy. My hope is that my children grow up to be respected in the industry as my father was and as I hope to be"
-Lorenzo Lamas, Actor

"You know what we the Supremes did, we inspired people just by being what we were and what we were doing, what we were about at the time. I heard that Oprah Winfrey said that seeing the Supremes on the Ed Sullivan Show gave her the idea that she too can do something great. I hope that my being myself will inspire other people and the main thing is that I'm a happy person and I hope that is what my legacy is. 'That's what a happy person looks like', even with all my flaws."
-Mary Wilson, Singer

"You know the Ministry is something I do, its natural. I moonlight as a grill salesman. I'm a full-time Preacher of the Church of Lord Jesus Christ, I love that. You don't want to become famous for that, the most famous one has been resurrected, Lord Jesus Christ. I'm not trying to be big anymore, it's an honor to be a human being. I would like to have it said that I donated to a college, one of our scholarships afforded someone to become a Howard Cosell or an Einstein"
-George Foreman, Two Time Heavyweight Boxing Champion

"I hope that people consider me a great ambassador to the sport. Somebody with great personality, generosity, brought more eyes to the sport of billiards, developed more for kids, and brought more attention to kids. If I could just make more people just love what I do and be an inspiration and at the end of the day I just want to be liked"
-Jeanette Lee, Professional Billiards Player

"A couple of pixels, if I can be just a pixel that'll be good. I am fascinated by the internet and by the changes in the film industry because we are going in a very different direction. The film business we are moving into very different territories we are reinventing film and we have to and I'm looking forward to that and I'm trying to be part of it. It's about pixels of light, it's about those machines there. It's no longer about film, film is going to go slowly. If you look at it now you can take that camera and film a movie and it'll cost you nothing. It gives us more competition, it opens up many windows and opens up for more crap but this is where new filmmakers come from. We're moving into a different direction and we should embrace that"
-Rutger Hauer, Actor

"When I think of legacies I think of what's going on tomorrow. I hope that people buy my books, I hope people laugh at my jokes. I hope that my daughter is happy. I hope that my husband and I have a good time"
-Rita Rudner, Comedian

"I'm pretty sure when it's all said and done there's a song 'Some Gave All' a song I wrote about a Vietnam veteran. I made it back in 1989. It ended up being the title of my first album. If you come to one of my shows you'll see that the signature song is 'Achy Breaky Heart' but the song that is really really touching people's lives and the song I'll be remembered for is 'Some Gave All'. I received a Bob Hope Congressional Medal of Honor for that song and the song is in the VFW Hall of Fame. I think that 'Some Gave All' will become the song I will be remembered for"
-Billy Ray Cyrus, Singer, Songwriter

"That my daughter still loves me, she's pretty proud of me, seen all of my work. She's a gifted girl herself, a woman. I have it made, a good brother, a mom that's 99 years old. I have a family that'd be the envy of any other guy's family,

they say 'oh Burt we know you're a tough guy, you lived a tough life.' What are you talking about the only tough part was when I left home!"
-Burt Young, Actor

"I hope that in the area of people saying the show seemed unique. My father used to say something is unique or it isn't. I hope that people liked the show and learned something"
-Dick Cavett, Television Host

"That I survived, I'm a survivor. I got through it and I just love to laugh. Look who I'm with, one of the funniest men in the world. That I got through it and I love it more than anything in the world"
-Tai Babilonia, Professional Figure Skater

"I hope I can improve myself in many ways as a human being, as a person, as a voice. Once you become a celebrity you get all these labels that you're really not and it's a responsibility"
-Davy Jones, Singer

"I don't think of the legacy. I don't think 'this movie was one of the greatest that ever happened'. I think I made a movie that works or it doesn't work"
-Eli Wallach, Actor

"I don't think in terms of a legacy because it's not how I'm wired. If I can help preserve and keep alive the music that is so important to me to the next generation and keep it going, I would feel like I did something significant"
-Michael Feinstein, Singer, Pianist & Music Revitalist

"He came and he tried"
-Carl Palmer, Drummer for the bands ELP and Asia

"Just the fact that I've passed through this life and made a mark on this life maybe not so much for myself but for others. Young girls and boys tell me all the time Miss Ralph I love you, you did it for me. And that's a great thing because I can go on in them. I know they'll mention my name and that feels incredible to me"
-Sheryl Lee Ralph,   Actress

"On my tombstone, I would love 'She lifted people's lives, including Harry's'"
-Carol Channing, Actress

"Oh my, is there going to be a legacy? Just to be a part of the Honeymooners, a part of TV history"
-Joyce Randolph, Actress

"That she gave a lot of entertainment to a lot of people and that they enjoyed seeing me. That they enjoyed my books particularly 'Miss Fortune's Daughters'"
-Joan Collins, Actress

"That I was of some use"
-Danny Glover, Actor

"One of perseverance, survival, strength, eternal youth, and eternal joy for the performing arts and gratitude of being a part of it and being part of a little history"
-Irene Cara, Singer, Actress

"I hope that people that have seen my work, because the immortality is there, thank God we have cinema because when we're gone people can be like hey look at that, hey not bad. When people see or remember my work, I hope people see an attempt at being honest about revealing emotions and feelings and attitudes of being a human being"
-Ben Gazzara, Actor

"I hope that people should not be dismissed because of their age, weight, background, the fact that they don't have any hair and whatever else I had to drag through life. I hope that I am living proof that you shouldn't dismiss them"
-Julian Fellows, Screenwriter

"She NEEEEEEEVER gave up"
-Melba Moore, Singer, Actress

"I hope that I'm not working forever but I would like to work as long as I possibly can. It's good to have my body as my instrument because it's incumbent upon me to keep it in good shape and keep it toned. I think I'll be able to sing till I'm well into my 80s. I think by the time I say bye-bye I'll be taken a bit more seriously than I was in the sixties"
-Lesley Gore, Singer

"I just hope people remember me for what I've done and what I've accomplished. And take what I've done and accomplished and use it for their own use. Because if they have the determination and desire they can do whatever. If I can come from Georgia dropout of high school and become successful then they can do it too"
-Larry Holmes, Professional Boxer

"Just that I made people happy with my music or touched them or lifted their spirits"
-Jordan Knight, Singer/Songwriter, Member of New Kids on the Block

"The only thing I want people to say leaving the theater is, 'Baby, I had a really good time'"
-Maurice Hines, Dancer, Choreographer

"Unimpeachably probably. Gold stars... I don't know. A good actor ultimately"
-Ed Asner, Actor

"Well, that's hard for me to say. For the most part, I've made music that uplifts people and if you think you are making a difference that will really inspire you too. I don't know exactly how I want to be remembered but my children love my music and Gloria [Richardson], I've been the only singer on this planet for Gloria and that means a lot to me"
-B.J. Thomas Singer

"She never met someone she couldn't like eventually, it just takes me some time to break them down"
-Sally Struthers, Actress

"That I understood the most tender sides of this art form and that I sung the sweetest songs"
-Melissa Errico, Singer, Actress

"I hope my legacy will be along the lines of Martin Luther King, Gandhi, Mother Teresa, and Malcolm X, and all the great people who strived to make the world a better place"
- Hailie Sahar, Actress

Recently, during an interview with celebrity journalist Eileen Shapiro, who was writing an article on me and the approaching 500th episode milestone for *Profiles*, she turned the tables on me and asked, 'Mickey what do you hope your legacy will be?' I answered…

"I just hope that after producing 500 episodes over twenty years, that I've entertained people, educated people, and most importantly, along the way, perhaps we've inspired people to be better"
-Mickey Burns, TV Host

Chapter 15
Epilogue

I'm sitting in my office on Staten Island, just a stone's throw from the Staten Island Ferry, reflecting on my life in sections. First growing up in the South Beach Projects, then finding sports as my way out; to my thirteen years as a high school basketball coach at McKee High School on Staten Island, which I retired from in 1988. Then on to my broadcasting career, which I still work at and cherish today.

Most of my reflection centers around feeling blessed. Every phase of my life has been extraordinary. If I had it to do all over again, I wouldn't change a thing. I have lived a dream existence and continue to do so today. Someone once told me 'Better lucky than good.' I'm not sure which one best fits my journey, but I do feel sometimes you have to be lucky; however, when you are, you also better be good at what you're doing.

I've always felt that life is short, so from a very young age, I decided not to do anything I didn't have a passion for. I don't ever remember getting out of bed in the morning without a passion to pursue my dreams and goals. I think that comes from growing up as a kid from the projects, constantly seeking approval, while always trying to prove to everyone that you're good enough and that you measure up.

I think back to my days at Missouri Valley College. When I first arrived I thought everyone was different, until I realized it was me who was different with my thick Brooklyn accent. I was taking a public speaking course at Missouri Valley with Professor Jack Sutton who said to me, 'Mickey, you don't pronounce your ERs or THs.' What he meant was, instead of enunciating power, I would say powa. I was leaving out the ER at the end. Instead of saying 'that', I would pronounce it as 'dat', no TH sound. I had a thick New York accent and was never aware of it. Where I came from everyone talked like that. After Professor Sutton recorded me, I understood what he was talking about. Once aware, I've been working on that accent ever since.

I've been on television in the New York Tri-State region since 2003. Wherever I go people stop me on the street or in the subway and comment, such as: 'I caught the episode the other night with Deepak Chopra, it was great.' I can't tell you how much these interactions have meant to me. I guess I'm still that kid from the projects seeking approval. Getting it means the world.

Since *Profiles* premiered on the NYC Media Network in 2003 we have produced over 450 episodes. To me, each one has been like a term paper. When I finished one interview, it's immediately on to the next one. Right from the start, preparation has always been the key to any success I've had as an interviewer. I felt this way as an athlete, as a coach, and currently as a television host. I don't feel you can ever be over prepared. Conducting a thirty-minute interview is not as easy as it sometimes appears. To make it interesting and compelling takes research and preparation. I spend an average of 10 hours doing research and formatting each interview. I can't tell you how many of my celebrity guests have complimented me for this over the years. The lesson here is, how do you get to Carnegie Hall? The answer is Practice, practice, practice. And how do you become a good interviewer? The answer is, Preparation, preparation, preparation.

The other day I drove past the South Beach Projects, which I hadn't done in years. They appeared shabby and run down. The playground and ball fields were empty, not like the old days when kids were playing everywhere. For me, it was like the ending scene from the film, *Titanic*, when an older Rose reflects back at the beauty and elegance of that grand ship before it sank to the bottom of the Atlantic. That's how it was for me, as I reflected back to the simpler times when kids could just be kids.

No drugs, no guns, just hundreds of kids playing the sport of the season, together!

So now I've written a book, which I thought would be impossible for me to ever achieve. However, during my interview with former host of *The Gong Show*, Chuck Barris said to me, 'Mickey, I think you have a book in you,' to which I responded, 'But I don't think I'll ever find the time.' Chuck laughed and said: 'Write one page a day, by the end of the year you'll have your book.' I didn't take his advice, because once I start writing I can't stop. I ended up writing in clusters, usually ten to twenty pages at a time. He did motivate me, however, and now I do have my book.

As for *Profiles*, on October 7th, 2017 we celebrated our 400th episode with an interview with the most famous face in daytime television history, Susan Lucci. And recently we made it to 450 episodes, with our eyes and passion firmly etched on reaching the 500 episode club. A reporter recently asked me what I credited the show's longevity to; my answer was, 'It's been a combination of having a dedicated staff while giving our audience long-form discussions with show business icons they just can't find anywhere else.' I meant that sincerely, but the truth of the matter is that we all love what we do. *Profiles* has been a passion for all of us involved with the show.

Over the years I've had so many great guests on *Profiles*. Today, I'm often asked, 'Who are some of the guests you still aspire to have on the show?' That's a valid question; in fact, I always have a list posted on the wall next to my desk that includes the top five celebrities I hope to have on *Profiles* someday. The current list looks like this:

1. Tom Jones. I've always been fascinated with his talent and longevity.
2. Rachel Welch. Eternally beautiful and intelligent, the ultimate female guest.
3. Pete Rose. Everyone wants to know about his gambling that's kept him out of the Hall of Fame.

   4. Angelina Jolie. Beautiful, talented and complex. I've always been impressed by her humanitarian efforts.

   5. Tom Hanks. Talented and down to earth. Everyone loves Tom Hanks, including me. I would love to profile his prolific career.

In my 2017 interview with actress Susan Lucci, I mentioned that on *All My Children*, Erica Kane had been married seven times, and I asked her, 'Was Erica Kane lucky or unlucky at love?' 'I think she was lucky for a while,' Susan responded with a big smile and a laugh. I then went on to say, 'Our viewers will be happy to learn, then, unlike Erica Kane, Susan Lucci has been married just once.' Lucci's had a long and successful marriage to Helmut Huber that includes two children and three grandchildren. When I mentioned this in our interview Susan said: 'It takes a village to be successful.' It certainly does! Guitarist Malina Moye calls that village her tribe, I call it my team. It includes family, friends, clergy, producers, network staff, videographers, sound and lighting technicians, photographers, editors and all the people that support you through the ups and downs of business and life, and ultimately always have your back. Not everyone fits into that team, but those whom I've let in have earned my loyalty and respect for the entire journey. Understanding the value of your village, tribe or team is certainly one of the keys to success regardless of one's chosen profession. It's been a grand and wonderful journey, and I feel so blessed that God has allowed me to take it.

Chapter 16
Acknowledgements

I would like to thank my partner Edwina Frances Martin for her undying love and support. Roy Menton for giving me my first on air opportunity at Time Warner. Arick Wierson, Diane Petzke, and Janet Choi - General Managers during the years of *Profiles* at the NYC Media Network. Mike McKenna. Roland Le Breton, Creative Director.

To NYC Council Member Debi Rose (D) of the 49th District serving the North Shore of Staten Island for her guidance, friendship and support. Former Staten Island Borough President Ralph Lamberti for your lifetime of guidance and friendship. Former Fox Anchor Bill McCreary for mentoring me from the start. Wayne Miller and Al Lambert for always being there. The *Profiles* Team Gary Humienny, Mario Launi, Michael "DiscoMike" Park, Shani Mitchell, Masieneth Ouk, Jorge Guzman Cruz, Rafael Munoz, Caitlin Tepper, Robert Braunfeld, Jeff Smith, Marlie Hall, Desi Sanchez, Laura Ameruso, Erica Martinez and Jay Alvear for helping make *Profiles* the best it could be. Producer/ Editor Extraordinaire Monina Montenegro for being my right hand for over 20 years, your loyalty & friendship has been remarkable and treasured. Hannah Madlansacay for her masterful edits and Little Sumo for letting her.

Lydia Loscalzo - Limos by Lydia, for transporting our celebrities to our set for over two decades. Hair Stylist Doreen Pedreira for taking care of my hair for over two decades. Snug Harbor Cultural Center for being our base of operations for over 20 years. Artie Colgan and Donald DeVincke for providing Security. Iroquois Hotel General Manager Robert Holmes, Brandon Gallagher, Garrette Ziem for making the *Profiles* Team part of your family. Gabriela Scott, Sales and Marketing Manager at the Algonquin Hotel. Ray Longobardi Owner of Pebble Creek Golf Club.

My golf buddies and close friends Jimmy Scara, Ronnie Farina and Richie Murphy for keeping me sane, making me crazy, and always laughing while losing my money.

I'd like to recognize my high school football Coach Sal Somma for giving me unlimited life skills, and Bob Steele former Athletic Director at McKee High School for giving me my first coaching opportunity back in the early 1970s. Missouri Valley College President Bonnie Humphrey and her right hand Eric Sappington for helping me return to my college roots. Monsignor Walter A. Birkle. Father Roy Cole at St. John's Episcopal Church. My mother Dorothy for making me the gentleman I aspire to be. My father Mickey Sr. for teaching me his street smarts and my brother Mark. My daughter Katie who makes life and all holidays special.

Lastly, to the nearly 500 celebrities who gave their time and energy to appear on *Profiles*… Thank you!

Photo Credits

Singer Chubby Checker & Dog The Bounty Hunter   Courtesy of Robert Braunfeld

Actor Robert Wagner   Courtesy of Robert Braunfeld

Kenny G   Courtesy of Robert Braunfeld

Actress Susan Lucci   Courtesy of Shani Mitchell

Actress Ming Na & Lou Diamond Phillips   Courtesy of Robert Braunfeld

Singer Meat Loaf   Courtesy of Robert Braunfeld

Singer Don McLean   Courtesy of Jeff Smith

Actress Tia Carrere   Courtesy of Robert Braunfeld

Singer Bill Medley   Courtesy of Robert Braunfeld

Deepak Chopra   Courtesy of Jeff Smith

Ballerina Misty Copeland   Courtesy of Robert Braunfeld

George Foreman   Courtesy of Robert Braunfeld

La Toya Jackson   Courtesy of Robert Braunfeld

Engelbert Humperdinck   Courtesy of Robert Braunfeld

Darryl McDaniels (Run DMC) & Hollywood Casting Director Sheila Jaffe   Courtesyof Robert Braunfeld

Singer Tony Orlando   Courtesy of Jeff Smith

Singer Darlene Love   Coutesy of Shani Mitchell

Charlie Daniels   Courtesy of Robert Braunfeld

Leslie Caron   Courtesy of Robert Braunfeld

Cover Photo, Mickey Burns - Courtesy of NYC Media

Back Cover, Mickey Burns - Courtesy of Dorothy Burns

Photo of Joan Rivers - Courtesy of Quest Media Entertainment, Inc.

Photo of LeRoy Neiman, Mickey Burns and Joe Namath - Courtesy of Quest Media Entertainment, Inc.

Photo of LeRoy Neiman & Muhammad Ali - Courtesy of Quest Media Entertainment, Inc.

Photo of Muhammad Ali & Mickey Burns - Courtesy of Quest Media Entertainment, Inc.

CPSIA information can be obtained
at www.ICGtesting.com
Printed in the USA
JSHW010734251019
2062JS00001B/1